Psychedelic
Sacred Sexuality

Psychedelic Sacred Sexuality

Explorations to Ecstasy and Oneness with Your Lover

Astraeus Amori

For information about this title or to order other books and/or
electronic media, contact the author at: astraeus@psychedelicsacredsexuality.com

Published by Pleiadian Portal Creations

ISBN (Paperback) 979-8-9898901-2-5
ISBN (eBook) 979-8-9898901-3-2

Printed in the United States of America

Cover Artwork by Autumn Skye, Titled: "Beloved."
Image used with permission. https://autumnskyeart.com/

Charts by Benjamin Malcolm PharmD.
https://www.spiritpharmacist.com/site/about

Summary Charts of Psychedelic Properties
by Ben Malcolm Pharm D.
https://www.spiritpharmacist.com/site/about

Artistic custom Illustrations for the book by Ewa Gawlik.
Instagram: @gawlikewa.

Photos and AI images by author.
Additional photos are licensed stock photos noted in references.

Contact Info:
Email: info@psychedelicsacredsexuality.com
Website: https://psychedelicsacredsexuality.com

Acknowledgements
and Dedication

In appreciation to the Indigenous shamans who have brought so much healing to the world through their plant medicines, and to the psychedelic researchers, chemists, and explorers who created unique molecules also aimed towards human healing and enlightenment.

Deepest appreciation to my family, friends, and my office team who have supported me personally and professionally.

And thanks to my book cover artist, Autumn Skye.

Also, I want to express gratitude to my book coach and editor, Elizabeth Ann Atkins, co-founder of Two Sisters Writing & Publishing®.

And finally, to Bella — my psychedelic companion who traveled through the deepest realms of loving oneness and ecstasy— whose presence has illuminated the path to the beauty and power of sacred sexuality.

May the sacred realm of shamanic and psychedelic medicine awaken our hearts and illuminate the path toward a more joyful, loving, compassionate, and harmonious world.

Contents

Disclaimer:

The educational information presented on this website and in this book revolves around a diverse range of plant medicines and synthetic molecules. This book does not consist of any specific medical or mental health advice to you. The purpose of the book is to explore the potential of various substances to enhance spiritual growth and intimacy within a trusted partnership. However, it is crucial to emphasize that participating in psychedelic medicine journeys together should only be undertaken after reasonable individual exploration with each compound within a safe set and setting.

Both partners should individually strive to gain competency, knowledge, and a stable flow of experience with each compound before proceeding. Furthermore, it is imperative to establish full consent from both partners, along with clear boundaries, before embarking on intimate journeys together. We strongly recommend that partners have a stable, loving, trustful, and supportive relationship of six months or longer prior to engaging in psychedelic journeys together. This recommendation extends to individuals in the LGBTQ+ community, polyamorous relationships, and other supportive, trusted relationships.

Additionally, it is important for both partners to be aware of potential plant-plant, drug-plant, drug-drug interactions, as well as psychiatric and medical contraindications. We advise consulting with a psychedelic medicine pharmacist or physician if there are any questions or concerns prior to proceeding. For individuals who are older or who have cardiovascular risk factors, it is recommended to undergo heart screening before engaging in these experiences. If you have psychiatric, neurological, or chronic medical conditions, such as bipolar, epilepsy or diabetes, it is essential to consult a physician who is open to psychedelic medicine and able to comprehensively assess your health risk factors before proceeding.

Of course, if you are pregnant or concerned about the possibility of being pregnant, psychedelics should be avoided. Psychedelics should also be avoided during breastfeeding. It is also strongly encouraged to consult with your psychiatrist, therapist, or plant medicine facilitator to seek their guidance and support throughout your adventure together, particularly in the intention (preparation) and integration (post-journey) process. In addition, you acknowledge that you should seek independent medical advice from a qualified professional to determine if you are medically cleared to engage in activities related to plant medicines and synthetic molecules. This team-based, comprehensive approach will ensure the safest and most beneficial outcomes for you.

The book and website contain discussions of psychoactive plants and synthetic molecules, including insights from field research conducted in parts of the world where the use of such substances is lawful. However, it is crucial to note that most of the psychoactive plants discussed in this book remain unlawful under U.S. law, with a few states having decriminalized their use with specific limits on possession and use. Under no circumstances should this book be interpreted as a recommendation or advocacy to break U.S. law. Furthermore, it should not be viewed as an endorsement by members of the psychedelic medicine community to experiment with psychoactive plants and synthetic psychedelic molecules.

The author and publisher are not encouraging, instigating, inciting, criminally facilitating, soliciting, or promoting any illegal activity. It is your responsibility to be informed about the legal status of any substance you use, if any. You understand and agree that the author and publisher are not making a recommendation that you engage in any specific experience or any illegal activity.

You are aware and understand that there are many serious known and unknown risks associated with engaging in the use of plant medicines and synthetic compounds, including that engaging in such use is a potentially dangerous activity that includes, but is not limited to, the risks of serious injury, disability, death, and/or property damages, as well as other forms of damages, losses, or personal injury, such as mental health, emotional, psychic, or other injuries (collectively, the "Risks").

We embrace and recommend all harm reduction techniques in the MAPS Zendo project (https://zendoproject.org/resources/), especially a safe set and setting, full consent with your partner/partners before and during journeys, awareness of drug-drug, plant-drug, and mental/physical contraindications to psychedelics, which should be discussed with your providers before proceeding.

By purchasing the book and/or reviewing the book's website, you expressly waive and release any and all claims which you may have, or which you may hereafter have, regarding the risks, whether known or unknown, against the author and publisher and its owners, officers, directors, managers, employees, agents, affiliates, members, successors, contractors, and assigns, arising out of or attributable to you use of plant medicines or synthetic compounds. You forever release and discharge the author and publisher from liability under such claims. In no circumstances shall the author's or publisher's total liability exceed the total amount paid for the book.

Any statements or claims about the possible benefits conferred by any process, services, or product referenced in this book have not been evaluated by the Food & Drug Administration unless otherwise expressly indicated (e.g. certain limited findings from FDA-approved clinical trials). Opinions, comments, and/or statements made by the author have not been evaluated or approved by the FDA, the AMA, or any other federal, state, local, or private agency unless otherwise expressly indicated (e.g. certain limited findings from FDA-approved clinical trials, or the relevant regulatory agency).

Each reader or user is solely responsible for his/her/their own health and wellness decisions. Therapies, products, services, or other information discussed are not offered to diagnose or prescribe for medical or psychological conditions nor to claim to prevent, treat, mitigate, or cure such conditions, nor to make recommendations for treatment of disease or to provide diagnosis, care, treatment, or rehabilitation of individuals, or apply medical, mental health, or human development principles.

If you have any disease, illnesses, are pregnant, or simply desire to improve your health and/or wellness, you must seek the advice of a medical doctor for medical advice, treatment, and services. No reader is establishing a doctor/patient relationship with the author by reading this book.

Instead, the discussions within the content serve an informational and educational purpose only, designed to promote further scientific research and advance conversations around enhancing relationships, spiritual growth, and the legalization of psychoactive plants for medical, spiritual, and safe personal therapeutic use. Given the widespread use of these plants and molecules, we believe that open discussions can promote more research, community feedback, and the development of enhanced safety protocols. While research and our personal beliefs support the safe use of psychoactive plants and synthetics for healing, they should be used, if at all, only in lawful circumstances, preferably through a qualified professional in the proper safe set and setting.

Vision, Perspective, and Opportunities:

We remain hopeful that the scientific, medical, spiritual, philosophical, religious, and regulatory communities will seek to understand psychedelics from both clinical perspectives (in treating depression, anxiety, PTSD, and addiction disorders) and their profound impacts on fostering love, compassion, and interconnectedness. The ripple effect of individual benefits expanding to couples, groups, and the community has the potential to shift consciousness and promote sustainability on our planet through improved collaboration rather than division.

It is evident that the rising violence in society is often a result of disconnection, fueled by technology and polarization. Greedy and power-hungry politicians and corporate billionaires are continuing to destabilize the world even more. Perhaps they need this medicine more than any other sub-group.

Looking at the big picture, it's nonsensical and reckless that U.S. society has allowed frequent, inappropriate, over-prescribing of a host of highly addictive opioids produced and influenced by the hugely for-profit pharmaceutical industry leading to an average of over 80,000 deaths annually from opioid-related overdoses. Simultaneously, our country continues to minimize DUI penalties, and the treatment of alcoholism, leading to an average of 140,000 deaths annually per CDC. More than 480,000 deaths a year are attributed to cigarette smoking, and sadly, gun-related deaths contribute to almost 50,000 a year, per CDC.

Harm reduction needs to center around these top three epidemics, but instead, lobbyists are dictating a different reality for the health and safety of our nation. Oh, and by the way, there have been no documented deaths directly related to a psilocybin overdose. No one would dare drive while deep in a psilocybin journey, but perhaps on a very rare occasion, they might do something careless like crossing a busy road and injuring themselves.

In contrast, psychedelic therapy has been shown in recent research to reduce alcohol and narcotic addiction, while at the same time potentially improving brain health through enhanced neuroplasticity, brain-derived neurotrophic factor stimulation, creativity, and compassion towards one another. All with minimal to no chance of overdose and death.

While the possibility of a 'bad trip' or adverse reaction exists, such outcomes are rare and largely preventable with proper guidance, awareness of contraindications, and a carefully curated set and setting. For some individuals, even after exploring various forms and dosages of psychedelics, the experience may not harmonize with their energy body or resonate with their psyche. In this case breath work, sound healing and other modalities can still allow one to travel deep into sacred sexuality.

In summary, psychedelic medicine offers a potential means to reconnect, heal, and rediscover love and respect for one another with the hope of mitigating some of society's dysfunction. The growing interest and use of integrative, functional shamanic medicine, meditation, yoga, and similar practices in society reflect a strong need for rebalancing as we navigate a world increasingly driven by artificial intelligence and the evolving trend towards singularity. These mind-body therapies, particularly psychedelic medicine, can help preserve our true human essence. I am hopeful that psychedelic medicine will be safe, affordable, and sustainable for broader benefits across all socioeconomic realms.

We wish you the best in your travels to deeper realms of love. This book and the corresponding website have been created from a heart-centered approach aimed at improving everyone's health and spiritual growth. Please feel free to email us if you have insights or recommendations in regards to the website or the book. I hope you enjoy this second edition. I'm committed to continually refining and enriching it based on the thoughtful feedback I receive—feel free to share your insights with me via email." We hope to enhance this book in future editions to come.

Introduction

Thank you for your interest in reading a book about interdimensional sexual flow!

Elements of adventure, boldness, creativity, and passion are needed to pick up a book of this nature and I congratulate you for doing so.

The goal of this book is to help you find a natural, sacred sexual flow with your partner or spouse that is not clouded by reading complicated books on tantra, but by giving you simple tips and ideas on how to take it to a higher level with psychedelics.

chose to write this second edition within a year, inspired by the valuable and heartfelt feedback I received. Navigating the intersection of psychedelics and sacred sexuality is no easy task. It's a complex, often controversial terrain filled with strong convictions and deep, multidimensional perspectives. My goal remains to offer the most accurate, responsible, and heart-centered guidance possible to help others heal and love one another more deeply. I will continue to refine this manuscript as I learn more from my inward work, my relationships, and constructive feedback from others.

I want you to see and feel your partner's chakras and to learn how to radiate your light into them. As you assist each other in healing, awakening, and intimate flow, I am hopeful that you will ultimately both experience oneness. Sometimes it will all align magically, while other times there may be some hiccups. What matters most is enjoying each other in a deep way without expectations and letting the process organically unfold by itself.

The content in this book is for the more "seasoned psychonauts" who are in a stable, trusted relationship that will seek full consent and communicate any boundaries before embarking on a higher dimensional journey together. ("Seasoned psychonauts" are those who have worked with psychedelics for at least a year or longer.) If you are in the early stages of psychedelic exploration, be sure to find the necessary time to independently work with a facilitator or therapist prior to diving in with your partner. Inward-directed self-work will help clear your field of negative energies and balance yourself to be with others in a more harmonic relationship.

This book is for everyone with an open mind, who is heart-centered and loving. Straight, LGBTQ+, and even those who claim to be from another planet, are all welcome. While I'm a heterosexual male, I am welcoming people of all backgrounds and orientations to enjoy an equally powerful experience. This, of course, includes any gender identity, sexual orientation, race, spiritual beliefs, or cultural background. The professional sketches were made to illustrate different poses for your benefit. While they are heterosexual and may not represent your body type or race you desire, the purpose is simply to give you the information you need without an intention to discriminate. However, please be sure to read the details in the disclaimer regarding risks, contraindications, etc., before proceeding on any adventures with your partner or partners.

It took three years for me to make the bold decision to write this book, and over 20 years of working with psychedelics—along with many years helping people as an integrative medicine physician (merging modern medicine with natural healing techniques)—to feel competent enough to discuss this subject matter. Intuitively, and from my heart, I felt the need to share my profound experiences to help others on their journey.

The book discusses varied ways to enjoy psychedelics with your partner in a safe set and setting. The major plant medicine and modern psychedelic molecules are discussed in terms of their effects on neurotransmitters and the physical and emotional sensations expected. A chart at the end of each of the major psychedelics is included to summarize and provide more scientific information for the geeks reading this book.

After discussing the various psychedelics, I share some of my personal erotic experiences of flowing into a blissful state, and state of oneness, achieved with my partner. My apologies if some of the stories are more or less graphic than you may desire or if you don't resonate with the images. Sometimes it's a challenge to find the perfect amount of detail in an erotic story to share. I also hope to illustrate the intersection between science and spirituality in this book. My thoughts may vary from others who write on the subject of sacred sexuality and tantra, but it is important for all of us to create a non-judgmental, collective consciousness on this subject, and recognize varied perspectives.

Take home the elements from this book that resonate with you, and let go of sections that don't. Psychedelics are not for everyone. Some may find focusing on meditation and breathwork as their best route to awakening. Feel free to agree/disagree with any of my insights or opinions and share your perspectives in a respectful, conscious field to help all of us grow spiritually. We are here to co-create and collaborate to manifest a better world, not to go after one another, especially in this realm.

My intention is to promote a deeper level of love, respect, and compassion for one another as we are all doing this deep inward work. We must learn to let go of our ongoing divisions and aggressiveness in our divided country and world at large. I seek to heal that wound with my time left on this planet, and to whatever degree is possible through everyone experiencing more authentic love.

Finally, from the depths of my heart, I wish you and every one a life filled with more compassion, coupled with a spiraling of your hearts together, enabling you to radiate this frequency to others, around Gaia, and the universe surrounding us.

Wishing you safe, blissful travels to the higher dimensions and back home.

—Astraeus Amori

Chapter 1

The Journey to
Sacred Sexuality

Many of my friends often ask, "How on earth did you develop such diverse interests in healing modalities, international cultures, archeology, shamanism, energy medicine, astrophysics, tantra, and more?"

Or, "Dude, what planet did you come from?"

The answer stems from my deep curiosity about how we got here, and how our universe and the field of energy surrounding us were created. Also, my inquisitiveness around why some humans are heart-centered and loving, while others are not. Add in a bold spirit of adventure and perseverance and you can find some level of understanding of why I've written this book! Lacking this weirdness, I'd probably be writing about something mundane like "Ketogenic Diets for a Sexier You!"

Travel really opened me up and sparked my thirst for knowledge in so many realms. Beginning as a globetrotter in my teens, I've had the chance to venture across more than thirty countries and immerse myself in diverse cultural beliefs surrounding spirituality and healing. By far, my most awe-inspiring experiences have been when I stepped out of my comfort zone and offered my help to underserved areas as a volunteer in Nepal and the Ukraine.

It's not simply about hiking through picturesque Himalayan landscapes and checking a trek or climb off my list, it's about making a meaningful impact in the lives of those I encounter in medical camps. The people I've met internationally have taught me so many valuable lessons about the resilience of the human spirit and the power of spirituality to transform lives. These unique experiences have left an indelible mark on my soul and ignited a passion for exploring shamanic healing.

During one of my medical volunteer trips to Nepal way back in 2000, I decided to take a day off from seeing patients and explore the vibrant cultural heritage of Bhaktapur, located just south of modern-day Kathmandu. I'd heard rumors of Tibetan merchants selling exquisite Thangka paintings and the intricate carvings adorning the temples piqued my curiosity. The architecture there reflects a rich history of Newari, Hindu, and Buddhist cultural influence.

As I wandered through the cobblestoned streets, I stumbled upon a temple unlike any I had seen before. Beautifully carved tantric figures in the gables and posts of Nyatapola Temple, Bhairava Temple, and Dattatreya Temples fascinated me.

Nyatapola Temple, built in 1702 AD, is dedicated to the goddess Siddhi Lakshmi. It is renowned for its five-tiered roof and intricate wood carvings. The intricate wood sculpting on this temple and the others depict various Tantric deities, symbols, and motifs that are considered to be among the finest examples of woodcarving in Nepal. Some of the temples date back to the 12th century AD.

This unexpected discovery reminded me of the rich cultural diversity that exists throughout the world, especially in Southeast Asia, and how each community expresses itself in unique, beautiful, and often sensual ways. It was a humbling reminder of the importance of keeping an open mind and being receptive to the unexpected.

Why would these beautifully carved, sexually explicit wooden figures adorn a temple? Clearly, the temples were dedicated to goddesses and gods based on their aesthetic flow and beauty. Sadly, anything explicit and culturally complex in the United States found publicly would be quickly taken down by the religious right, the emerging cancel culture, or stolen by thieves looking to sell it in the black market. Amazingly, all of it remained unharmed in Nepal until catastrophic earthquakes in 2015.

Further travels to Cambodia, Thailand, Vietnam, and India showed me how prolific this beautiful art is worldwide. Clearly, the intention is to honor the merging union of the sacred divine feminine and masculine energies for spiritual enlightenment. This sacred union has been artistically represented in temples not just for hundreds, but often for thousands of years! These clearly are sacred carvings, and not pornographic carvings that many uneducated or religiously biased Westerners view them to be.

In modern cultures, particularly through religious oversight, these images have been censored and demonized. Furthermore, we have relegated sex to be simply procreation or viewed superficially as a pleasure-oriented endeavor. The lost practice of sacred sexuality must be renewed if we truly seek spiritual enlightenment and a societal trend towards higher states of consciousness. While this practice is not for everyone, even a small ripple of this consciousness can make a difference.

Tantric art on a temple at Patan Durbar Square, Nepal.

Our country experienced a short period of sexual freedom in the '60s and '70s that was accelerated with access to improved birth control and psychedelic enlightenment, including ecstatic states of oneness. Protests to the Vietnam War, along with escapism through psychedelic journeys, were needed for many to process the dark reality of daily body counts being reported from a war that never should have happened. Music festivals emerged and the hippie movement climaxed in Bethel, New York, with the three-day Woodstock music festival in 1969. Many feel that the heavy use of psychedelics kept the music goers in flow with the music and surrounding energies despite the heat, humidity, rain, and mud everywhere. Most commonly, LSD was enjoyed, given its easy availability and affordability as it flowed from underground labs in San Francisco. Weed and magic mushroom use was common too, but they were unfortunately followed by cocaine, opium, and heroin.

Quite the contrast to today's arid and dusty Burning Man event on the other side of the country in the Black Rock Desert of Nevada. Well, that is until Burning Man turned into the "Mud Man Fest" of 2023!

While I don't feel many of those at Woodstock were by any means consciously seeking deep spiritual insights, I do believe that many inadvertently experienced enlightened states with the application of psychedelics. Oneness happens on psychedelics. Thank you, Terrence Mckenna, Timothy Leary, Alexander Shulgin, Ram Das, and many others for helping so many find oneness and a deeper connection to nature and ourselves through the promotion of psychedelics! It is through this inward and outward loving work that others may become more engaged in protecting our planet and assisting in so many other humanitarian efforts worldwide.

Since the '60s, we transitioned away from this unified and brief psychedelic movement, as it was quickly and reflexively reined in during the '70s by religious leaders, politicians, and others who desired a more conservative cultural norm and to control the masses. President Richard Nixon enacted the Substance Abuse Act in 1970, which criminalized psychedelics, in an effort to shut down massive protests and free-thinking, which was catalyzed by their awakening to the reality of the Vietnam War and other unethical governmental actions.

The '60s through '80s allowed for a reasonable level of sexual freedom, but this trend reversed as the fear of HIV/AIDS emerged in 1981.

The three-year Covid pandemic (March 2020–May 2023), along with Trumpism, led to isolation and increased political divisions over vaccinations, masks, quarantines, etc., creating a further observable decrease in human socialization, and simple friendly social interactions. Trump's behavior made many believe it's okay to be a jerk, amongst many other unethical behaviors! Social media lit up with unvetted fake posts and conspiracy theories from our adversaries, designed to divide us and destabilize us even further. This divisive rhetoric continues to increase as our country hasn't found a way to heal itself by understanding one another and attempting to find common ground in the middle. Fast forward to 2025 and we are seeing even further division combined with a disruption of our financial markets, judicial system, immigration, health care and more. Not to mention Doge (Department of Governmental Efficiency) lay-offs by oligarch Elon Musk.

Post-pandemic, I witnessed so many strangers avoiding eye contact and preferring to walk around fixated on their cell phones. I still ponder how much of this behavior arose from cell phone addiction versus the ramifications of pandemic isolation, reduced socialization, and even political polarization. Likely a combination of all this, with layers of stress related to uncertainty of our future due to climate change, concerns of nuclear war, and ongoing global instability.

Having emerged from the challenging times of this three-year pandemic, while also seeing rising division in our country and the world, we find ourselves isolated and seeing more people of all ages struggling with anxiety, depression, rising suicide rates, homicides, and mass shootings. Isn't it time for us to come back together and love one another? Even today, I continue to be disheartened by ongoing observation of minimal eye contact and smiles towards one another, simple awareness of each other in public spaces. Heads are increasingly buried in phones, and it feels like I'm walking amongst zombies most days in the city! While I don't feel everyone needs to say hello as they pass by me, a simple gaze and smile reassures me that I am passing a conscious person.

Yes, I have hope for a better future, but we need to first relearn how to be human and connect with one another and nature again! Moving forward, let's find a sustainable path of collaboration and consciousness, instead of blaming each other for anything and everything. Reassuring trends of light have been emerging despite the frequent dark clouds over the last few decades.

The emergence of yoga, and the yoga lifestyle, is a good example. While it was obscure in the '50s, it soon became more mainstream with yoga studios in the '70s and is now a ubiquitous and mainstream activity. Every summer that I attend mindful music festivals, yoga is an integral part of them. Meditation, conscious relating workshops, ecstatic dance, permaculture and other amazing topics and activities are woven into the schedule. While I have no interest in the megapolis Burning Man event, I do enjoy the smaller, mindful-based music festivals, and mini-burn events. There I can connect with like-minded souls without the guilt of a large carbon footprint event that includes endless lines of cars entering the Black Rock Desert, overflowing porta toilets, and overflowing egos saying, "Ya know, this is my tenth burn."

Recent books, including Michael Pollan's "How to Change Your Mind,"[1] focused on psilocybin (magic mushrooms) benefits, and Paul Stamets' "Fantastic Fungi" (2019) book and movie[2] helped peak interest in the medicinal benefits of psilocybin.

In November 2022, my home state of Colorado passed Proposition 122[3] which decriminalizes many plant medicines. Thanks to the more progressive community here, in Oregon, as well as other states, moving in this direction, we may be entering a psychedelic renaissance as more people can enjoy plant medicine and additional research can be performed. Slowly, but safely and cautiously, we hope to bring psilocybin, MDMA, and other plant medicines into the safe and legal therapeutic setting to treat depression, anxiety, addiction disorders, and PTSD. Most importantly, it has been shown to be more effective than many traditional pharmacological approaches.

In August 2023, a study showed the benefits of even a single dose of psilocybin in the treatment of depression. Myself and other progressive physicians/providers are hopeful that the transition from decriminalization to legalization will happen in the coming years, and feel that the combination of the non-clinical (underground facilitation) with clinical will provide broader accessibility to all socioeconomic levels to access the healing benefits of psychedelics. Legalization nationwide would be amazing, but will likely take another decade to demonstrate responsible use and therapeutic benefits to do so.

As a psychedelic community, we must commit to long-term collaboration, compassion, understanding, reciprocity, and love for one another to accelerate this movement. Being respectful to Indigenous communities and finding ways to collaborate for the greater good of our planet that honors all, should be our goal. We also recognize that virtually every race and culture has had a dark past at some point, and we should not villainize someone for something that happened generations ago, that they had no control over. We truly must all walk our talk on unity, and avoid discrimination against each other regardless of skin color, culture, religion, age, education, social, or financial status.

Speaking of coming together, psychedelics are showing ongoing evidence to improve human compassion, socialization, and connectedness to nature,[4] and may even reduce criminal behavior.[5] I've heard many people joke that we could change the world by enriching the water for a week with LSD!

We must help those who are stuck in the shallows of this materialistic, three-dimensional world and help them see the higher dimensions to give us long-term, healthy sustainability, and an improved opportunity to avoid global annihilation by nuclear war. This enhanced altruistic responsibility will hopefully create guardrails around artificial intelligence going rogue, as well.

The short-term profit mentality of Americans being applied by investors, oil companies, big pharma, developers, the agrochemical industry, and others will hurt us all in the long run. We must help awaken them to the sustainable altruistic vision and implementation. I'm simply referring to what is often called a "conscious business model." While some of my opinions may be controversial to some, I want the reader to grasp the larger perspective. I'm one who enjoys hearing all perspectives, and I hope you do, too!

What does all this have to do with sacred sexuality, you ask?!

The answer is simple. As you awaken through sacred sexuality, discovering a deep love for yourself and others, you will help create a conscious society and a field of energy that will awaken those around you. We are struggling to reach a tipping point of collective high vibrational energy and the world needs your help.

Are you in?

Are you ready to enjoy a sexual relationship with your partner that can facilitate awakening, mind expansion, and an amplified flow of energy? Then I dare you to read on!

So, What is Sacred Sexuality?

Sacred sexuality refers to the spiritual aspects of sexuality, where sex is seen as a sacred act that can be used for spiritual growth and transformation. It is often associated with various spiritual practices, such as Tantra, Taoist sexual practices, Kama Sutra, and Shamanism, that emphasize the unity of body, mind, and spirit.

Sacred sexuality is not just about physical pleasure or procreation, but involves a deeper emotional, mental, and spiritual connection between partners. It involves developing an awareness and reverence for the body, the senses, and the divine energy that flows through us. The flow in this space will make you feel more alive and hyper-connected to your lover beyond imagination.

In this realm, sex is seen as a way to connect with the divine, to experience the oneness of all things, and to achieve higher states of consciousness. It can be practiced alone or with a partner and it involves exploring and honoring one's own sexuality, as well as the sexuality of others. Spiraling divine feminine and masculine energies to higher vibrational states amongst a couple is part of the practice.

Various practices, such as meditation, breathwork, energy work, tantric massage, and plant medicine can be alchemized with sacred sexuality to help you further awaken and channel sexual energy in a positive and transformative way.

The Roots of Sacred Sexuality

The roots of sacred sexuality began in the ancient tantric traditions of India and Tibet. In India, it's believed to have begun in roughly 500 BC and, over time, the tradition traveled to the north and was adopted by Tibetan Buddhism around roughly 700 AD before expanding further into Nepal and Southeast Asia. Tantra is aimed at cultivating awareness and awakening consciousness. The following is a complex tantric word salad, but it's important to grasp the history and variations.

The types of Tantra can be broadly categorized based on their religious and cultural contexts:

- Hindu Tantra: This is one of the oldest forms of Tantra, deeply rooted in Hindu philosophy and practices. It encompasses a wide range of rituals, meditation techniques, and yogic practices aimed at spiritual liberation (moksha), and the realization of the divine. Hindu Tantra often involves the worship of deities like Shiva and Shakti and includes various schools like Kashmir Shaivism and Shri Vidya.

- Buddhist Tantra (Vajrayana Buddhism): This form of Tantra is integral to Tibetan Buddhism and is known as Vajrayana. It includes advanced meditation techniques, visualization of deities, mantra chanting, and ritualistic practices. The goal is to rapidly achieve enlightenment by harnessing sensual energies including, but not limited to, sexual energy. Vajrayana is known for its iconography, which sometimes includes symbolic sexual imagery representing the union of wisdom and compassion.

- Jain Tantra: Less well-known than its Hindu and Buddhist counterparts, Jain Tantra incorporates mantras, rituals, and symbols into the Jain spiritual practice. It is more focused on protection, healing, and purification, rather than on sexual practices.

- Modern Tantra/Neo-Tantra/Western Tantra: A blended adaptation of traditional Eastern Tantric practices, often focusing more on the sexual aspects. It emphasizes sexual wellness, intimacy, and spiritual sex, often detaching from the more complex spiritual and religious elements of traditional Tantra. It's often associated with the teachings of Osho and other New Age gurus and emphasizes the integration of spirituality and sexuality. This type of Tantra aligns best with the context of this book.

- Left-Hand and Right-Hand Tantra: These terms are often used to distinguish between different approaches within Tantra. Left-Hand Tantra (Vamachara) is more unconventional, sometimes involving taboo-breaking rituals, including sexual practices, while Right-Hand Tantra (Dakshinachara) emphasizes more orthodox and symbolic practices without physical sexuality.

Each of the above types of Tantra has its own set of practices, beliefs, and goals, as they are often interwoven with the cultural and religious fabric of the societies in which they evolved. While Tantra in the West is often synonymous with sex, in its traditional forms, it is a profound and comprehensive spiritual path involving much more than just sexual practices.

Here is a bit more of a breakdown of the elements that Neo-Tantra (Modern Tantra) weaves into a practice of sacred sexuality.

- Sexual Wellness and Exploration: Emphasizing sexual exploration as a path to personal growth and spiritual enlightenment. It includes practices that enhance sexual pleasure, intimacy, and the connection between partners, thus enhancing your overall wellness, too.

- Spiritual and Physical Union: Viewing sexual union as not just a physical act, but also as a spiritual and emotional one, where partners can achieve higher states of consciousness and oneness as they weave their divine feminine and masculine energies together.

- Mindfulness and Presence: Being fully present during sexual activities heightens awareness and connection to the experience. Psychedelics help to further facilitate being present, as it takes the default mode network offline and can place you in a timeless state.

- Energy Work: This may include balancing chakras, placing crystals on your lover, and flowing energy through Tantric massage/bodywork. Partners seek to cultivate Kundalini energy for each other.

- Breathwork Techniques: May be incorporated to enhance relaxation, connection, and energy flow. This can include alternate nostril breathing, holotropic breathwork, etc.

- Sexuality is treated as sacred, a departure from many Western attitudes that might view sex as simple gratification with only the orgasmic end point in mind.

- Inclusiveness: Neo-Tantra is typically inclusive, and open to people of all sexual orientations and relationship models.

Please keep in mind that Neo-Tantra is distinct from traditional Tantra, which is part of a complex spiritual tradition in Hinduism, Buddhism, and Jainism, and involves a wide range of practices beyond just the sexual. Traditional forms of Tantra involve a deeper, more philosophically rich practice often encompassing meditation, yoga, rituals, and a holistic approach to life.

Here's more on **Hindu Tantra** and the deities often cited.

In Hindu Tantra, Goddess Parvati holds a profound pantheon-like position. She's revered as the divine consort of Lord Shiva and together they are often viewed as the ultimate representation of cosmic union and balance of divine feminine and masculine, united as the androgynous form of Lord Ardhanarishvara.

Shiva and Parvati symbolize the fundamental principles of the universe: consciousness and energy, stillness and dynamism, transcendence and immanence.

Goddess Parvati

Lord Shiva

Shiva/Parvati=Lord Ardhanarishvara

Additional major Hindu deities include:

- Kali - a fierce goddess associated with destruction and transformation.

- Tara - a compassionate goddess associated with healing and protection.

- Durga - a powerful goddess associated with courage and strength.

- Ganesh - A popular deity associated with wisdom, good luck, and removing obstacles.

Hindu (Indian) Tantra is often subclassified into White Tantra, Red Tantra, or Black Tantra.

White Tantra is associated with various schools of Hinduism, Buddhism, and Sikhism and involves the use of specific postures, breathing techniques, visualization, and meditation practices. This can then be channeled into sexual energy in a way that promotes spiritual growth, healing, and awakening. In a higher realm, this sexual energy connects to the divine, leading to enlightenment.

It may be practiced with your partner, solo, or in a group.

Practiced with you and your partner's intentions, applied techniques can be channeled into sexual energy to promote a deeper connection, healing, and spiritual growth together. Specific postures, breathing techniques, and meditation practices may be used together to facilitate flow.

Going solo allows you to work on your own sexual energy through solo meditation, visualization, and breathing exercises, typically in private and incorporated into your spiritual practice.

In a group setting and under the guidance of a teacher, participants engage in various exercises and rituals designed to facilitate the flow of energy and enhance spiritual awareness. Group energetic coherence can amplify your individual experience.

White Tantra is sometimes linked with Right-Hand Tantra (Dakshinachara), which uses symbolic rituals and does not involve physical sexuality. It's best to seek guidance from a qualified teacher or mentor when exploring the various forms of Hindu Tantra.

Red Tantra is another branch that is often associated with sexual practices. While White Tantra focuses more on enlightenment, Red Tantra embarks more on the physical and sensual aspects of existence. It incorporates sexual energy as a means to achieve spiritual enlightenment but does so through direct physical experience and the exploration of sensuality and intimacy.

Red Tantra practices often involve a partner and include specific sexual rituals, energy exchanges, and guided exercises aimed at heightening sexual and emotional connection. The goal is often to transcend the physical act of sex and find a deeper, spiritual connection through it. Red Tantra is often misunderstood and misrepresented in Western cultures, where it's sometimes associated with purely hedonistic or promiscuous behavior.

However, for those who practice it with intention and commitment, this more mainstream and accepted form of Tantra can be a powerful path towards spiritual growth and self-realization.

Black Tantra, also known as dark tantra, is a spiritual practice that is often associated with using sexual energy for power and control rather than for connection and union with others.

I advise that you completely avoid this type of Tantra, and any other forms of manipulative, dark spiritual or religious practices. It's being mentioned for you to gain awareness and to steer clear.

In Black Tantra, the focus is on manipulating sexual energy in order to achieve certain goals, such as personal power or material success. It's sometimes used to describe a more extreme or unconventional form of Tantra, which may involve practices such as sex magic, or the use of taboo or forbidden practices.

Unlike other forms of tantra, which emphasize the importance of love, connection, and spiritual growth, Black Tantra is often seen as a more manipulative and self-centered practice.

Some practitioners of Black Tantra may use certain rituals or techniques, such as visualization or breathwork, to tap into their sexual energy and direct it towards achieving their goals.

Please note that most practitioners of Tantra do not engage in Black Tantra. Many practitioners view it as a perversion of the true teachings of Tantra, which emphasizes the importance of love, connection, and spiritual growth.

In fact, sacred sexuality is based on a very different set of principles and practices that blends the best tantric elements: Neo-Tantra, White, Red, Tibetan Tantra, and Kama Sutra.

Tibetan Tantra

How does Tibetan Tantra to the north of India, differ from the Hindu type? From Tibet, three classes of Tantra emerged: Kriya Tantra, Charya Tantra, and Yoga Tantra. These three classes all represent a progressive series of practices leading to higher states of realization.

Tibetan Tantra focuses on "deity yoga," which involves visualizing oneself as a deity and then engaging in practices that are designed to transform one's ordinary perceptions into those of a deity. This helps purify the mind, channeling one to higher states of consciousness.

It places more emphasis on the use of mantra and ritual than Indian Tantra, and a guru is seen as a crucial guide and mentor from whom one can receive teachings and initiations along the path.

The Yab-Yum represents the fusion of the masculine (Yab) and feminine (Yum) energies.

It's believed to represent the unification of all dualities, leading to a state of enlightenment.

Also a symbol of spiritual transformation, its practice is associated with the highest levels of tantric teachings.

Yab-Yum embrace.

In summary, Indian, Tibetan, and Neo-Tantra have collectively contributed to the evolution of today's theories and practices of sacred sexuality. Both Neo-Tantra (Modern Tantra) and sacred sexuality emphasize egalitarianism and inclusivity, supporting those in the LGBTQIA community and are in general fairly similar. Sacred sexuality places more emphasis on surrender and submission to the divine while flowing into states of oneness, staying in the field of light, love, and compassion.

Are bondage activities OK in sacred sexuality?

Bondage may even be used with clear communication and consent between partners in sacred sexuality, to improve intimacy, channel sexual energy, and achieve a deeper spiritual connection with one's partner. No one should be hurt, of course, and boundaries must be respected based on initial and ongoing re-consent. Allowing vulnerability in the context of full consent maintains the sacred sexuality container.

It's important to note that in the context of sacred sexuality, bondage is typically approached with reverence and respect. It's not seen as a purely sexual act, but rather as a way to access higher states of consciousness, trust with your lover, and connect with the divine.

Again, consent and communication are prioritized, and partners should consider a spiritual verbal agreement or understanding before engaging in any kind of bondage or BDSM practices.

In this way, the practice emphasizes the importance of love, connection, and the sacred nature of human sexuality. Again, rather than seeking power or control over others, practitioners of sacred sexuality seek to deepen their connection with their partners and with the divine through sexual union.

Now let's explore how we can integrate this into our lives!

Chapter 2

How Can We Awaken Ourselves through Sacred Sexuality?

Most of us would never think of sacred sexuality as a modality toward awakening. Instead, we'd be more likely to mention activities such as meditation, prayer, religious rituals, a guru, a trauma/crisis, breathwork, psychedelics, or yoga being the usual modalities to get there.

The beautiful thing is that these more common modalities of awakening can be stepping stones leading us down the trail to the powerful dimensions of sacred sexuality. Like many things, it's a synergy of spiritual practices that will lead us down the trail to further enlightenment.

What attributes will you need to enhance your ability to awaken through sacred sexuality?

The first attribute is being open-minded.

Being open to infinite possibilities in our universe allows one to gain broader and deeper insights during meditations and lucid dreaming. Keeping an open mind also enhances the frequency of synchronicities. You'll be amazed how many more people you'll run across who share your vision and or simply want to be friends because of your more open, loving field of energy. If your partner struggles to be open-minded like you, there's still hope. Try to get them engaged in mindful-based activities such as breathwork, to allow them to experience the deeper realms of their energy body.

If that's not helpful, consider a week or longer plant medicine retreat. Many of us have been programmed to be hypercritical of the mystical and spiritual, and need our brains stirred up like a snow globe with psychedelics. By this, I mean shaking things up in a way that the brain is defragmented and re-patterned to be more appreciative and less resistant to varied perspectives. So, when they say, "I don't believe that there's such a thing as an auric field," reply with something like, "I'd love for you to be open to the possibility that an auric field exists, and someday, science may actually be able to confirm it."

As we age, we lose neuroplasticity and it takes more work to re-wire ourselves and others to be more open-minded to concepts in energy medicine, etc. Oftentimes psychedelics can facilitate this neuroplasticity we used to have during our youthful years. Neuroscientists like to define much of this more precisely as "metaplasticity." Metaplasticity is the idea that the history of synaptic activity (neuron connections) can affect the synaptic strength's potential for change in the future. This concept is an extension of the idea of synaptic plasticity, which is the ability of synapses (the connections between neurons in the brain) to strengthen or weaken over time, in response to increases or decreases in their activity.[6]

Psychotherapy can impact neuroplasticity and possibly metaplasticity, but to a lesser degree than psychedelic therapy. Combining both will yield the greatest outcomes, which is why I always encourage integration and ongoing therapy as needed.

While we can't push our partners or friends to do this deeper psychedelic work, perhaps by sharing your passion around the subject, they'll move from a contemplative mode into action mode. If your partner doesn't want to follow this path with you and you feel held back, perhaps it's time to move on. Give your partner adequate time and space to evolve, but at some point, whether it is months or years, you will know intuitively if it is sustainable.

This happened to me, and while it was very challenging and I waited years, it allowed my ex-wife and I to continue in directions that were in the highest alignment with our soul's path. We remain close friends and are both much happier after moving forward. While I feared the ramifications from my family and my kids, I was amazed at how they were supportive once they understood why we were going in different directions. Your ongoing open-mindedness will help source in a new partner, often through synchronicity, to join you in your journey into sacred sexuality.

The second attribute is to be open-hearted, compassionate, and willing to flow into unconditional love.

Having a closed heart chakra and lacking compassion for others will make it very difficult to move forward with your lover in this realm. If you've suffered traumas that have blocked your heart chakra and your ability to have empathy and compassion, then it's time for you to seek help and clear these fields before moving forward. Oftentimes a skilled and balanced partner can help you with some of this, but other times, seeking out a therapist or trauma therapist who can do EMDR, breathwork, Reiki and other modalities can help.

MDMA (Molly) with a skilled therapist/facilitator can also help dramatically, but it can take multiple sessions with this molecule to clear blockages and open one's heart. It's best to address and move on from a trauma as quickly as you can. Otherwise, it's a thorn in your side, creating ongoing stress and inflammation. Find a therapist who can help you work through it efficiently rather than dragging the process on unnecessarily. I have seen this happen with many of my patients, and I'm not saying a Tony Robbins approach is needed, but I'm recommending a balanced and effective approach that, if possible, should include MDMA.

Another important element within this virtue is self-love. One has to let go of the shame of not being perfect and recognize that you and all of us will make stupid mistakes, or get into unfortunate situations beyond our control. That's part of being human. We must let go of the past, live in the present, and love ourselves and others to do this work.

The third attribute is to strive for a balanced energy body.

Depending on the cultural and spiritual perspectives, one may describe this as balancing your chakras, optimizing Prana or Qi, achieving a luminous energy body, etc. This can be a challenge, as many of us will have blockages in certain chakras, such as the third chakra, where we hold fear and apprehension.

Engaging in yoga, meditation, breath work, Qi Gong, Tai Chi, and other energy-balancing activities can help flow your energy freely and allow your auric field to expand. As your chakras flow freely and your auric field radiates, you'll be able to merge and amplify fields with your lover to even higher levels together. An auric field is best described as radiant light around your physical body that can be perceived by individuals with special senses, and sometimes by others while on psychedelics. If you feel energy that's stuck in a particular chakra and you can't resolve this on your own, seek the help of an energy healer, shaman or acupuncturist.

Oftentimes psychedelics will allow you to feel your own chakras with your hands just slightly above them, and you may be able to sense and clear the blockage, sending it light or spinning energy into it. DMT has given me the most profound ability to do this for five to 10 minutes after "returning to earth." Sometimes San Pedro and Psilocybin can dial in this superpower for you, too.

Learn to feel the energy resonating from your palms and fingertips, creating a "Qi ball." Simply rub your hands together for 30 seconds, then feel the energy and heat between them, especially when they are about an inch apart. As you move your hands further apart, maintaining the sense of connection or tension between them, visualize the ball of Qi compressing and expanding with your hand movements. This helps to enhance your sensitivity to Qi and your ability to control it. As you practice this more, you can palpate a large ball of light energy between your hands. Now you have mastered an ancient Qi Gong practice!

Learn to then channel light from the stars and/or Mother Earth into your hands and along your chakras, so you don't deplete your own qi. My strongest flow of energy emerges from the center of my right palm, even though I'm a lefty. I often hold my left hand with a crystal in my palm to the sky, and bring in energy from Gaia through my feet while standing or through my root chakra while sitting. Soon you'll be doing energy work on others once you develop this skill. Get Reiki certified, or learn from other energy healers' advanced techniques, including how to protect yourself from dark energies and how to clear them.

The fourth attribute is Boldness.

We must be bold enough to engage in this creative and multi-dimensional world of energy flow. Not everyone is capable of adventuring into this realm. They fear losing control, experiencing the unknown feelings and sensations, and perhaps traveling inwards to learn more about themselves, or into the astral realms of oneness with all. You don't have to climb Mt. Everest on your first adventures with psychedelics and your lover, but you'll need to be willing to climb some smaller mountains for starters.

Sometimes, you'll take a wrong path and feel frustrated, but as you let go and try again, you both will find your way. No goals or objectives are needed, other than simply flowing in a state of deep love. Allow the rest to manifest along the way. If you need a guide to help you get started, find a therapist or facilitator to help you find your way initially, and then you'll develop the confidence to break trail on your own.

The fifth attribute is Trust and Vulnerability.

We have to develop trust in ourselves and others to do the deep work. Oftentimes we may doubt ourselves and our intentions. When this happens, we have to dissect whether the doubt is related to fear, or if it's a lack of confidence related to past failures or bad decisions. Creating intentions to move towards a field of trust is needed to flow into sacred sexuality and awakening.

As we develop greater trust in ourselves and our partners, we have to be willing to share our vulnerabilities. While this can sometimes be difficult for men making them feel less manly, the reality is, it will show strength in their willingness to do so. When we share our vulnerabilities with trusted friends, family, or partners, it opens us up to receive emotional support, sound advice, and other realms of help to make us stronger and healthier individuals. I've seen patients who do not want to share a diagnosis of cancer with friends and suffer in an isolated bubble. After I've encouraged them to share with close family and friends, the love and compassion channeled back to them helps take the cancer down.

Transforming oneself from victim to accepting the challenge to conquer can be the difference between being a cancer survivor versus heading to hospice. Sourcing in emotional and energetic support from others and the universe is key to anyone overcoming an illness or cancer. You have superpowers to deploy; don't dismiss them!

Sharing past sexual traumas or physical and emotional abuse can be even more difficult than sharing a life-threatening diagnosis. This topic is worthy of several books and a consultation with a professional trauma therapist. I am not attempting to comprehensively address this topic by any means. In general, a willingness to share these events with a therapist and/or your trusted lover or friend can be therapeutic over time. Ultimately as extremely difficult as it sounds, moving to forgiveness is needed to heal and to be present in the moment.

Yes, pretty much all of us have experienced some level of trauma. Even the royals. We don't want it to define our lives and we must seek ways to move beyond it into a state of happiness in the now. Again, one must let go and eject stuck, negative energy thorns to clear and heal. Ruminating over trauma in a victim mentality for years will just drive it deeper and create more opportunities for physical and mental disharmony. I strongly feel that MDMA therapy is the most effective way forward in difficult cases. Ketamine assisted psychotherapy is another effective option to consider.

Of course, there are other virtues beyond those I've mentioned to move you along the path to awakening. Please be sure to explore the wisdom teachings of gurus, shamans, spiritual teachers, religious leaders, and others who've shared their thoughts to the world. I'll provide links to some you might enjoy on the book's website. But remember, you are first and foremost your own guru.

Now that we've reviewed some suggested preparations for sacred sexuality flow, let's dive into modalities that can alchemize your flow!

Chapter 3

Alchemies for Sacred Sexual Flow

L et's explore romantic catalysts to enhance sacred sexual flow before we delve into adding the interdimensional enhancements of psychedelics!

Start by asking: What can I add to my bedroom setting that will further stimulate my sense of smell, taste, vision, touch, and hearing in a positive way?

Begin by creating a setting that feels perfect to the two of you. If you've already created an amazing sex room, then perhaps you're set to go. Congrats, you wild ones! If simply starting with your bedroom, let's look for ways to jazz it up! Create a quick list of creative things you'd like to see, feel, hear, touch, and smell. Have fun doing it, and if you don't have it in your dwelling or even your van, seek it out online or in a local store.

An Alchemy of Divine Masculine and Feminine Energies Uniting.

Touch

Your skin has an estimated five million sensory receptors. In this modern age, we sadly neglect those receptors. Many of us, men and women, hold back from hugging someone or even putting a hand on a shoulder due to the fear of being accused of inappropriate touch. Perhaps this human disconnect is even contributing to losing a sense of belonging, resulting in rising rates of depression, anxiety, suicide, or potentially leading some towards violent behavior. For this reason, I feel we need to give touch the greatest emphasis to rebalance ourselves and others. If you want to hug someone and it's questionable how they may respond, simply ask them if it's OK. I'm hopeful that hugs will become more socially acceptable as observed in the cultures of Latin American countries and southern European countries. Hugs would be an interesting variable for an anthropologist to analyze in regards to the frequency of violence in a country. Of course, political, economic, education levels, religion, access to guns, access to psychedelics, legal structure, etc. would also need to be in the equation, too.

A gentle kiss to your partner with slow lovemaking versus the more intense deep kiss and passionate primal flow are examples of varied levels of intimate touch we may desire. Oftentimes we dance these levels of intensity throughout our intimate flow together.

Even the bedding under you is important. Besides a comfortable mattress, having the texture of a furry, fluffy, or silky comforter and pillows helps create additional sensory input. Even the head and tail board can make a difference if you want something to hold on to, or perhaps tie your lover to!

Perhaps your partner enjoys the varied sensations of a tantric massage, an occasional slap on the ass with a small whip, or the sensation of a feather lightly coursing their back. Sometimes giving a primal deep loving hug and simply holding each other is more than enough to nurture our senses.

Quartz crystals can be amazing to apply to your partner's chakras on the front or backside. These can help open the chakras and often interconnect them better. If you are an energy healer, you can use your hands to spin more energy through them just above the crystals. One can acquire a quiver of seven crystals, or keep it simple with three crystals, using a small, walnut-sized crystal for the third eye, and a three- to four-inch-long one for the heart and root chakras.

Try gently laying on top of your partner to feel the crystals more intimately connecting the two of you. My favorites to work with are Lemurian, but any crystal that calls to you can work. Of course, there are some amazing gemstones shaped for the yoni and the butt if you desire more advanced crystalline flow! Warm your crystals and gemstones for comfort before using them, but warm them slowly or they may crack.

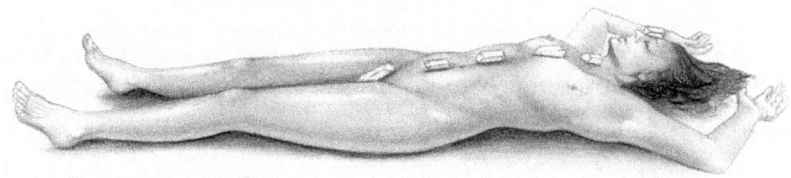

Quartz crystals applied to the chakras for energy balancing.

Sacred geometric forms can also be applied to chakras, or held in your hands meditatively. They can help entrain your brain and your energetic state into a higher dimensional realm as you gaze into them while in a psychedelic state. Applying them or flowing them in circles above the chakras can balance and help interconnect the chakras.

Balancing the third chakra with a sacred geometric dodecahedron form.

A powerful, gold-plated, sacred geometric form for energy work—
Dodecahedron with Icosahedron by buddhamaitreya.org
called the "Adams Grid."

Tantric massage is another deep and powerful way to share your sensual loving energy, so having massage oil or cream nearby is key, should you be called to enjoy this. It can be the perfect fore-play or a stand-alone activity to give and receive loving energy from your partner. For the more advanced, tantric massage can be done while making slow love while either one massages your back or chest, depending on your position. After making love, it can help the post-orgasmic energy flow, too. Sometimes I'll massage Bella on her ass and lower back while slowly making love to her from behind. Running your hand up her spine as she orgasms is other-worldly. Gals can do the same to guys with prostate G-spot butt play.

Tantric Massage.

If it's been an intense day, start with this to help you relax, and transition to love-making later with greater passion and heart-centered flow. Using your hands intuitively while seeking feed-back from your partner on pressure and location can be helpful.

CBD oil or cream can be especially helpful if the stress level is high and/or muscles are sore. I've found that intuitive flow is best, but you can always brush up on more advanced techniques by reading books and watching videos prior to embarking on this.

Be sure to also work your front sides by flowing beautiful circular energy into both women's and men's chest areas. Massage around the jaw, cheeks, forehead, as well as the scalp, as this can often be neglected. Working from the neck to the feet on your partner's back, don't be shy about flowing plenty of energy in the root chakra region, including the perineum.

You can get more advanced by setting up your side table with a hot stone massage warmer and a massage oil warmer. If you get a stone warmer, get one that you can dial up or down to a perfect temperature. Purchase gemstones that resonate with you. Obsidian, shungite, and labradorite are my favorites. The rainbow colors of labradorite with ambient candlelight are other-worldly, especially on psychedelics. Beyond holding the stones and massaging your partner with them, you can also place them on any part of the body simply to warm and balance energies.

Last but not least in the touch category—sex toys! If you feel drawn to them, start simple and expand out. Oftentimes you'll find yourself with a treasure chest of 12 or more, but usually, three to four will become your favorites. Lots of exploration is needed to find which ones provide the stimulation you are looking for, whether it's targeting the G-spot, clitoris, or anal stimulation. Guys may enjoy some of the more advanced prostate massagers for their G-spot stimulation. Sometimes using toys that are made from things like natural rose quartz is all you need, but of course, many higher-tech ones with multiple vibratory modes can take it up a few notches!

Storing all this fun stuff can be a challenge, and usually, you don't want it lying around for the mother-in-law or kids to find!

If you don't have drawers in your bedside table, you can find a nice box or two to hold all random goodies to slide out spontaneously from under your bed when called to play with one thing or another. I've often teased my lover about a Craftsman tool chest with drawers! There's no need to have an organized plan or list of things you plan to do, as that can take away from the playful flow. Just have easy, close access to them, so you don't run off searching for something in a closet, leaving your lover naked and frustrated!

Taste

Drinks and snacks are key. Keep it simple and small. A bowl of fruit and water is all you need. No need for a Super Bowl-type tray of snacks!

A small honey bear is always nice to squirt on your partner's body, and perhaps some whipped cream or dipping chocolate, too, when you want to tease your palate. Of course, sharing a pint of gelato after hours of sexual flow can be pretty orgasmic, too!

Yummy bedside treats for tantric flow!

Smell

Small aromatherapy bottles of your favorite essential oils are great to keep in the drawer. My partner and I enjoy the more earthy scents of Palo Santo, sandalwood, musk, Cap Neroli, and Patchouli. We even love the pheromones from one another's armpits! Aromatic essential oils can be amazing to play with when your lover is blindfolded. Rub the scent between your hands and let them breathe it in deeply, and dab a little on their third eye region or just under their nostrils.

Scented candles or incense work well to enliven your senses, too. I typically don't like to mix various scents and may stay with a sandalwood candle or a nag champa incense.

Visual

Lighting is important, too. Candles in a dim or dark room can suffice, but sometimes you may desire to have a remote-controlled astral laser-light projector! Light up the ceiling with nebulas and profound laser stars for a more trippy ambiance. These can be found for less than $100 online. Colored LED lights on plants or around windows can strengthen the ambiance depth, too.

You might say, "Whoah, so many options!"

I've laid out a buffet table of eye candy options, but again, choose nothing or whatever resonates with the two of you. Just feel into potential options of where you might want to travel with your lover on a particular night and how a particular plant medicine may or may not work well with it.

Maybe your bedroom is too mundane and you'd prefer a cozy love nest in front of a blazing fireplace with a glass of wine and cheese, or a hike out to a more primal setting with a blanket or yoga mat on the forest floor. Granite countertops in the kitchen or a cool concrete floor can be sexy on the other side of the spectrum, too! Be creative and change it up as you continue your journeys together.

Sound

I desire music roughly half of the time when I'm in intimate flow and 100% of time when I am in an intimate flow while enjoying psychedelics. When enjoying the natural ambiance of crashing waves, a cascading creek, or a crackling fire, music becomes an option, of course. Energetically aligned music, sung or played, and/or the sounds of nature can magically dance the energy of psychedelics, facilitating greater geometric imagery, and colors. This phenomenon—known as synesthesia—allows one to see color and images stimulated by sound. Sometimes one can smell and even taste shapes! Shipibo shamans sing icaros to enhance healing and imagery during an Ayahuasca journey. Rarely, some people will have these extra sensory superpowers without the application of psychedelics.

In terms of audio devices, a simple, well-charged Bluetooth speaker or an elaborate sound system for you audiophiles will do.

Other times, you may want to ditch the playlist to spin a crystal bowl, play drums, tap away on a hand pan, shake a rattle, play flute, play didgeridoo, or even play a violin if you're able to. I've found shamanic hand drums and rattles to be the easiest to dive into. Singing or chanting mantras can be a powerful modality that facilitates heart-opening and energetic balance.

Oming or humming over your partner's chakras can be an easy way to help facilitate chakra balancing, too. Check out Jonathan and Andi Goldman's book, *The Humming Effect*, for more on this! Sometimes we'll chant along with kirtan mantra music by artists such as Krishna Das, Snatam Kaur, and Deva Premal while hearing the accompaniment of beautiful instruments, voices, harmonium, and tabla drum.

Spotify has amazing playlists with tantric music, microhouse, EDM, mantra music, tribal music, romantic rock, and so many other genres to fit your mood. I've listed some of my favorite artists in the resource section of this book for you. Of course, you can create your own as you explore. I've created playlists for various plant medicines and a heart-opening playlist for MDMA that I love! It's important to freshen them up and ask friends to share their playlists for greater diversity and brain stimulation.

For each one of these sensory experiences, check in with your partner for their desires, finding the alchemies that feel perfect for both of you. Some may prefer 80's rock love songs over mantra music. In the next chapter, I'll share a short story as I integrate a few of these elements!

Chapter 4

Psilocybin, the Foundational Psychedelic for Sacred Sexual Flow

One of my favorite psychedelics for sacred sexual flow is psilocybin. In states such as Oregon and Colorado, psilocybin-containing mushrooms have been decriminalized or legalized, allowing many to cultivate and enjoy them without as much legal concern.

Psilocybin has been used for healing for over 6,000 years, and there's evidence that it's been used by humans on every continent except Antarctica. There are over 180 species identified at this time and some hypothesize that spores may have been seeded by asteroids hitting Earth billions of years ago. Pretty far out, right?!

This amazing fungus is one of the most sustainable, economical, and effective ways to enter into the flow of psychedelic sacred sexuality. It's safe, reasonably easy to grow, and easy enough to find a friend who grows to donate to your new endeavors. Psilocybin use may soon become as mainstream as Cannabis as states and countries recognize the mental health benefits and minimal risks associated with these special fungi.

Psilocybin is converted to psilocin after we eat it. This then activates serotonin 2A (5HT2A) receptors, leading to the altered state of enhanced visual imagery, colors, and sensation. Psilocin binds several other 5HT receptors and likely has effects on other monoamine neurotransmitter systems.

At a microdose (50 to 200 mg) of psilocybin mushrooms, you won't feel too much, but for most of us, going beyond one gram (1000 mg), we'll start to bring in subtle geometry and greater sensitivity to touch, sound, taste, and visuals. You may also experience heart-opening and a deeper connection to your lover. Some may have sadness and other emotions, and you may need to comfort each other by doing energy work, breath work, and sound healing, or simply holding space for the one who's struggling.

Psilocybin Mushrooms.

Microdosing is trending so much that I rarely find a day that I'm not asked about it by a patient, or see someone recommending it in social media. Microdosing is anecdotally a helpful modality for improving mood, reducing anxiety, and improving creativity and flow. Current research is limited, but has not yet demonstrated major benefits, and effects appear limited to dosing days. For most, trying it carries minimal risks, although persons may want to limit "courses" or cycles of microdosing to a maximum of three months to avoid unknown theoretical risks associated with 5HT2B receptor stimulation and Valvular Heart Disease (VHD).[7]

Until more research is completed, one could consider one of the many protocols, Fadiman, Stamets, etc, in which microdosers generally utilize schedules and catalysts (Stamets) to improve efficacy and reduce potential risk of VHD.[8] At some point, if you haven't, you'll need a macrodose (2.5 to 5 grams) to drop in with your partner in a safe, set and setting with intentions of simply enjoying and flowing into higher dimensions together side by side. Brain QEEG (electrical activity) is markedly increased after taking psilocybin in this image on the right compared to before psilocybin on the left.

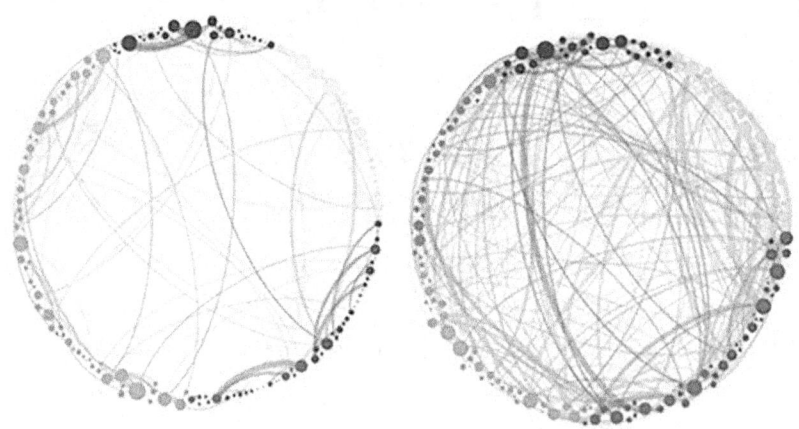

Brain QEEG before Psilocybin and during Psilocybin.
(Proceedings of the Royal Society Image)

Once you've done this several times, you may be called to experience it in the flow of sacred sexuality. Finding the dose that isn't too intense, but allows you to be present with enhanced sensation, along with light to medium geometry and color, is ideal. For me, that's typically in the one-gram range, since I'm more sensitive than most. Everyone varies on the dose needed and experimentation will be needed.

One interesting observation is that while I used to need higher doses in the three-gram range, I now need much less. Perhaps it is due to repetitive stimulation of neural tracts, where an individual's brain familiarity with psychedelic states leads to more effective responses allowing a lower dose over time. This is contrary to what happens to individuals taking SSRI antidepressants (and most other chronically administered psychotropics) where there is a decreased responsiveness and a higher dose needed after prolonged use. I've heard this from others, but would love more of your feedback, too. Sometimes I'll use the "lemon tek" procedure with psilocybin mushrooms to reduce nausea and accelerate the onset of the psychedelic experience. It basically involves sqeezing a lemon into a cup of ground mushrooms, and allowing it to sit for 30 minutes, facilitating the release of psilocin. This process can be viewed on YouTube (https://www.youtube.com/watch?v=T1LFPD8XVFk)

Once you both find the sweet spot with the right dose and species of psilocybin mushrooms, it's time to enjoy each other. Follow your intuition and flow your energy into your partner with tantric massage, if this feels right. Or maybe enjoy some foreplay with oral sex. This is a time to be slow and mindful, not a time to rush into an end game. Drip some honey on your partner, or perhaps some chocolate. Your taste is enhanced with these fungi, so turn your lover into a gourmet delight! Ask him or her what they want. Is the pressure good? Does the tempo feel right? Don't be shy. Psilocybin can lighten your shyness, making you more open to communicating what you really desire.

Sometimes you'll need to pause and simply hold each other; again, there is no hurry. Breathe and simply be. Passion will flow more deeply, and orgasms will be intensified as you savor each other slowly. Sometimes you will need to wait until you are beyond two hours to flow with it if a psychedelic is a bit overstimulating. Wait for the nausea and temperature variations to clear if they occur. The typical duration of a mushroom journey is around four hours. Again, simply enjoy being present in this slowed-down time together, and when the time feels naturally right, take your clothes off and have fun!!

A passionate, resonant, astral night in the mountains!

One snowy evening as we enjoyed a glass of wine after dinner, Bella and I found ourselves talking about the amazing resonant healing of Tibetan sound bowls. We'd been neglecting them for some time and had enjoyed many amplified erotic moments with them in the past.

"Let's grab the bowls and enjoy them fireside tonight!" she said. It had been a couple of weeks since we had last played them together in a meditative sound healing ceremony, but months since we'd used them in sacred sexual flow.

"Sounds great," I said. "How about we enhance our senses with a light dose of psilocybin too?"

"Mmm yes, Astraeus," she said. "I'll grab a gram for each of us out of the kitchen."

This weekend, we happened to be down at my mountain home in Telluride, Colorado, not far from the energies of the sacred ancient Pueblo site of Mesa Verde. I started a fire in the adobe fireplace with some split pine and scrub oak branches for kindling. Watching the sparks fly off the blue and yellow flames of the crackling fire was mesmerizing.

Heading back to my ceremony room, I retrieved seven brass Tibetan singing bowls to warm next to the fire, along with a few Lemurian crystals. The sun was setting over the San Juan mountains, and a beautiful Alpenglow illuminated the western faces of these majestic peaks. The old hammered Tibetan bowls gently reflected the glow of the flames onto the floor as we watched the sun set, and the stars emerge. We began to see enhanced detail in the logs, and more vivid colors emerged from the flames as our mushrooms began to kick in.

Bella left for a moment and came back with a couple of furry blankets. We laid one on top of two yoga mats and kept the other to drape across us to create the perfect fireside nest. Sitting there in a timeless field, we watched the fire together and allowed it to warm us from this cold winter eve.

Soon she pulled off her sweater, exposing her beautifully rounded breasts, allowing them to feel the primal heat of the burning logs in front of her. The curves on her breasts artistically linked to the curves of the bowls, and the rounded fireplace in this golden natural light. Seeing her dark hair cascading down her back, with the flames flickering in her pupils, seemed surreal. I just sat there absorbing the view as I would appreciate a sculpture by Rodin. But of course, this was much better.

Sitting behind her, watching the flames, I lightly massaged her neck and shoulders. Kissing the back of her neck, then her spine, I decided to have her rotate around, facing me with her back to the fire. Peeling my flannel shirt off and feeling her warm breasts on my chest was magical. We embraced and kissed lightly. Her spine was hot from the fire behind her, and I loved the heat on my hands as I held her. Deep, passionate kisses followed, and within minutes, we found ourselves lying naked and holding each other.

I laid her down on her back, then gently placed the warmed Tibetan bowls above her head on the floor, and one on her chest and pelvic region.

"Hold a crystal in each hand, and I'll place one on your third eye, Bella," I said.

After doing so, I chimed a smaller bowl above her head, resonating her crown chakra, followed by chiming and spinning the ones on her heart (fourth chakra) and pelvic area (second chakra). She smiled subtly and I could see her forehead and body relaxing as I continued to spin the bowls in a meditative, focused manner. Resonating the bowl on her chest, I could sense her heart chakra opening up more. Pausing for a bit, I leaned over to kiss and admire her beautiful breasts illuminated by the golden fire. Reclining back, I watched the fire dance before me as I continued to spin the bowls on her goddess-like body.

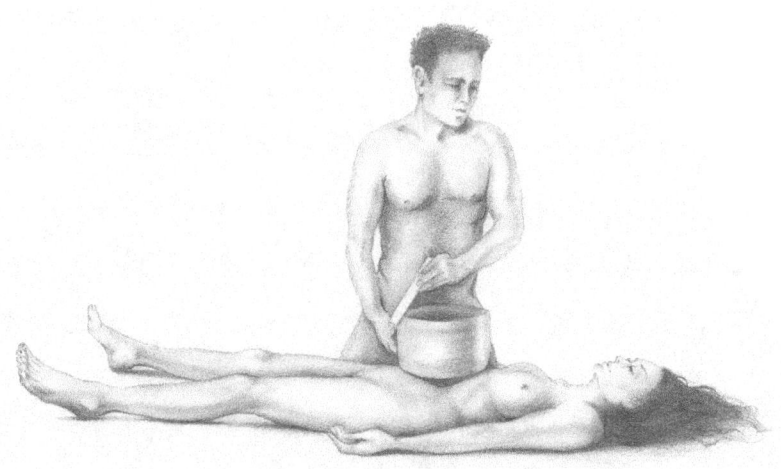

Spinning a crystal bowl on her third chakra.

Moving the larger C# bowl over her pubic bone region, I began to resonate deeper frequencies to energize her root and second chakra. Her hips began to slightly rotate back and forth as I chimed and flowed it into her, deeper and deeper. I had her move her legs apart slightly to then move the bowl low enough to resonate her yoni. Chiming the heart and crown chakra, followed by spinning the root chakra, I watched her auric field begin to glow. I stopped for a moment to add another couple of logs to the fire, knocking some embers free and watching them dance upward.

Positioning her into a downward dog position, I then resonated her root chakra by chiming the deeper-toned brass Tibetan bowl with the mallet several times.

"OMFG Astraeus," she said, "you're lighting my Kundalini energy on fire with all this sound healing!"

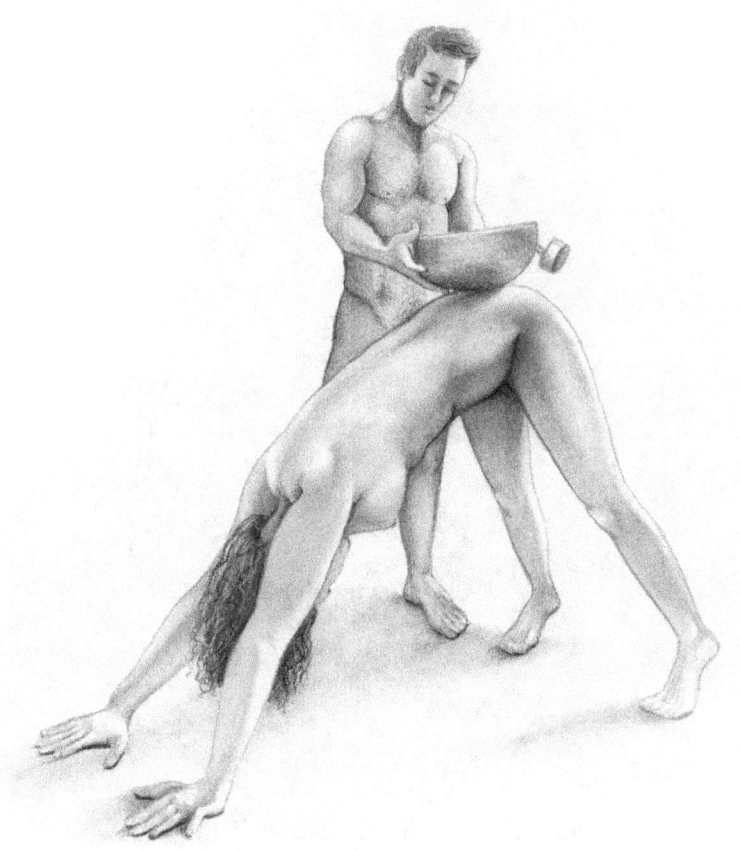

Tantric sound healing of the root chakra with a Tibetan bowl.

Sitting back down beside her, I guided her through several deep breaths with the bowls set by her side. Holding the central palm of my right hand just above her root chakra, then going progressively up to her crown, I flowed, opened, and balanced her chakras as needed. In areas that felt slightly cool, I spun more energy to balance them, then flowed the energy upwards, connecting them as I visualized rainbow light flowing into my left palm, and out of my right palm into her chakras. Placing my forehead next to hers, I could feel my third eye being gently electrified. I like to call this third eye kissing.

Connecting with your partner's third eye.

I then kissed her lips gently, followed by placing the large bowl back on her clitoris. Spinning it slowly, then more intensely, she began to moan and rotate her hips more upwards. Chiming, it created a shorter but more intense ripples of vibrations into her yoni.

"Loving this so much, Astraeus!" she said, moving the bowl a little lower. I positioned it a bit lower and spun the bowl faster, noting that she was so close to releasing.

"Go down on me," she said in a sexy voice. I moved the bowl away and began to kiss her navel. Soon, I slowly and intuitively caressed her yoni with the tip of my tongue, feeling her wildly release. Holding my third eye on her yoni as she breathed through the ecstatic release, I saw subtle geometry emerging like a lotus flower.

"Wow, so amazing to see so much geometry on a subtle dose," I said. "The energy between us amplifies the plant medicine effects!"

Heading north, I embraced her and gave her light kisses on her lips. I could feel her heart still pounding against my chest from the orgasm. Still wanting to be inside her, I decided to tease her with my tongue for two more orgasms, bringing her to a more heightened state. Nothing aroused me more than watching her orgasm with her beautiful ecstatic moans and the flickering light from the fire on her breasts.

Soon she rolled me on my back, and slowly guided me into her fiery wet yoni. Feeling so hard and sensitive, we began with a slow tempo, feeling our energies merge perfectly and flowing in perfect unison. Time stood still as we were in this state of sacred sexual flow.

Our tempo increased, and as I went deep, I made a subtle circular movement to tease her more. Loving that motion, I could feel her tension rising. Pausing occasionally to run my tongue over her lips, and passionately kiss her, we continued this timeless rhythm.

The blanket and hardwood floor underneath me felt perfect, allowing me to ground out as she rode me a bit faster and forcefully, pulsing me into Mother Earth.

I gripped her butt firmly, but let her control the pace and angle as she descended on me.

Holding back from releasing into her, we continued to spiral our energies upwards in our spines in a Kundalini manner. Feeling the energy rise intensely, towards climax at times, we'd slow down to savor being on the edge.

Soon I felt myself in another realm, watching her beautiful breasts bouncing and hair dancing around as she increased the tempo a few notches.

She began to moan with her eyes wide open, staring deep into my eyes, as I felt her contracting around me. Seconds later, we both released together for what seemed like eternity!

Bella remained on top, with me inside her as we breathed and integrated our orgasmic flow in a meditative way over several minutes. Laying down and embracing each other, we felt a deep sense of oneness.

"Bella, this was a deep and amazing night," I said. I love how we blended sound and plant medicine so seamlessly, amplifying our sexual flow tonight. Can't wait for our next loving adventure!"

"Mmm," she responded, "I'm craving a full day of this kind of flow with LSD for our next one, Astraeus."

"Can't wait, babe. Let's make that happen soon!"

Psilocybin Summary

How It Works

- Classic psychedelic tryptamine.

- Non-specific partial agonist at 5HT receptors, effects likely mediated by 5HT2A/1A/2C receptors although binds several other serotonin receptors 5HT/2B/1D/1E/7/6.

- Weak SERT, alpha 2A/2B/2C, and imidazoline 1 binding.

- Functionally selective partial agonism at 5HT2A receptors most implicated in psychedelic mechanism of action.

Metabolism of Psilocin and Psilocybin

- Rapidly dephosphorylated by alkaline phosphatase or non-specific esterase to psilocin.

- Psilocin is primarily glucuronidated by UGT1A10.

- Psilocin is partially metabolized by monoamine oxidase (MAO).

- Duration of psilocybin/psilocin is about three to six hours.

Typical Dosing

Used as either pure psilocybin or dried mushrooms (~1% w/w, variable species*).

- **Micro:** 0.5-3 mg Psilocybin or 50-300mg of Dried Psilocybin Mushrooms.

- **Light:** 10mg Psilocybin or 1 gm of Dried Psilocybin Mushrooms.

- **Moderate:** 20-30 mg psilocybin or 2-3 gms Dried Psilocybin Mushrooms.
- **High:** 30+mg or >3 gms Dried Mushrooms).

  *some strains of mushrooms may be considerably stronger than others; dosing of dried mushrooms are approximated.

Common Journey Experiences

- Empathogenic heart opening.
- Enhanced visualization of colors & sounds. Geometry is common.
- Enhanced connection to nature and to others.

Potential Therapeutic Uses

- Treatment-resistant unipolar depression.
- Depression and Anxiety associated with life-threatening illness.
- Demoralization in long-term AIDS survivors.
- Obsessive-Compulsive Disorder.
- Alcohol or Tobacco Use Disorder.

Potential Adverse Effects

Physical

Nausea
Increased blood pressure & heart rate
Discomfort

Psych/Neuro

Transient anxiety
Emotional discomfort
Paranoia or confusion
Post-use headache

Drug Interactions & Contraindications

Drug Interactions

- Lithium → Increased risk of seizures or dysphoric experience quality, contraindicated.

- Chronic SSRI/SNRI or MAOI use → Possible diminished effects.

- Buspirone → Possible diminished effects.

- Acute MAOI use → Intensified psychedelic effects.

- Benzodiazepines → Possible diminished effects.

- Atypical antipsychotics → Reduced psychedelic effects.

- Triptan migraine agents → Vasoconstriction and increased cardiovascular risks.

Contraindicated

- Bipolar I or severe bipolar conditions.
- Schizophrenia, psychosis, or psychotic conditions.

Legality

Psilocybin and psilocybin-containing products are regulated as illicit or Schedule I substances by the United States federal government. However, the legality of psilocybin is a rapidly evolving area and some states and local jurisdictions have passed legalization or decriminalization measures. Check the most recent laws and regulations in your specific jurisdiction to get the latest information on the legality of psilocybin.

- May 2019: Denver, Colorado, became the first city in the United States to decriminalize the possession and use of psilocybin for adults over the age of 21.

- November 2020: Oregon became the first state in the U.S. to legalize psilocybin *therapy* (regulated, licensed therapy sessions) through a ballot measure.

- The list of cities that have decriminalized the possession and use of psilocybin is growing and includes Oakland and Santa Cruz, California; Ann Arbor, Michigan; Washington DC; Somerville, Massachusetts; Detroit, Michigan; Seattle, Washington; etc.

Chapter 5

MDMA: The Love Molecule

MDMA is currently my favorite molecule to work with, but of course, this could change next month, trending me to loving San Pedro or another molecule.

MDMA (3,4-methylenedioxymethamphetamine), commonly known as ecstasy or Molly, is widely recognized as an extremely powerful molecule that can foster deep, heart-centered connections between individuals either in intimate or platonic relationships. Its profound effects have led many underground couples therapists to incorporate it into their practices, amplifying the outcomes of traditional talk therapy.

Furthermore, MDMA has shown promising results for treatment-refractory, post-traumatic stress disorder (PTSD) due to the dedicated efforts of organizations like the Multidisciplinary Association of Psychedelic Studies (MAPS).[9] Unfortunately and sadly, the FDA didn't approve the MDMA application by Lykos in late 2024, but I'm hopeful that with additional steps requested by the FDA, that it can be passed in a few years. The delay in approving this will result in further suicides related to mostly ineffective contemporary therapies for PTSD.

Speaking of, if you or your lover have a history of significant trauma (particularly of a sexual nature), or PTSD, it is best to work through this first before proceeding with MDMA together.

Finding a trauma therapist who works with MDMA and EMDR can be particularly helpful. Underground use will continue to be widespread due to its affordability, but please be sure to test for purity yourself or with your facilitator.

One of the differentiating aspects of MDMA is its ability to enhance emotional bonding and intimacy with minimal hallucinogenic changes to perception. Oftentimes it's more of a visual enhancement with improved visual acuity, and for some, an appreciation of auric fields noticing subtle colors of light around their crown, hands, etc. Adding one to two grams of psilocybin a few hours into the journey can enhance an MDMA journey bringing in geometry and more color.

Some prefer to front-end a journey with the psilocybin dose, but I tend to like doing it after Molly. This technique is commonly known as the "hippy flip." Another amazing and more profound combo, known as the candy flip, is to add LSD 50 to 100 mcg at the beginning or prior to ingestion of MDMA. Many prefer to add LSD 2 hours after MDMA roll. These combos should only be tried after gaining reasonable experience with both psychedelics alone.

The primary benefit of MDMA is its ability to profoundly increase one's sense of openness while also facilitating a strong desire for physical closeness to one's partner and others. This is what defines it as an empathogen. It is by far the most heart-opening molecule I have experienced.

Couples will share more openly what they desire, and how they feel about each other, thanks to the dopamine boost. Serotonin and norepinephrine levels are also increased by this molecule, creating the "ecstasy" experience, making you feel like dancing and moving!

Oxytocin stimulation enhances the deep bonding you will feel with your lover, making you want to hug them deeply and endlessly. The magical bumps in these neurotransmitters, combined with the well-crafted set and setting, creates the experience you'll never want to end.

Here's a little more detail on how MDMA impacts each of these neurotransmitters:

- Serotonin: MDMA primarily stimulates the release of serotonin. Increased serotonin levels contribute to the euphoric and empathogenic effects associated with MDMA. However, MDMA use may deplete serotonin levels in the brain, leading to fatigue, so a post-journey/roll protocol is recommended later in this chapter.

Dopamine: MDMA increases dopamine release, albeit to a lesser extent compared to serotonin. Dopamine is associated with feelings of pleasure, reward, and motivation. The enhanced motivation can encourage you to communicate deep thoughts (opening of your throat chakra) that perhaps you've held back on. Sharing loving, appreciative thoughts is always encouraged. The increased dopamine activity contributes to the euphoria experienced by some MDMA users.

Norepinephrine: MDMA stimulates the release of norepinephrine, a neurotransmitter involved in the body's stress response. Increased norepinephrine levels can lead to heightened arousal, as well as increased heart rate and blood pressure. These effects can contribute to the stimulant properties of MDMA. Note: Taking OTC Magnesium Threonate (Neuromag) can soften cardiovascular stimulation and muscle tension.

Oxytocin and Vasopressin, which are involved in social bonding and emotional regulation, are also increased, but to a lesser degree compared to the others. The oxytocin bump, along with serotonin, promotes most of the heart-opening effect. Sublingual or nasal spray oxytocin Rx can be added late in an MDMA roll to enhance or take the empathogenic effects even deeper.

Considering the impact on these neurotransmitters, one can see how activities such as tantric massage, energy work, couples yoga, passionate kissing, oral sex, and sound healing take on new dimensions and elicit indescribable sensations!

What's most intriguing to me is how my partner and I are naturally drawn to certain yoga-like positions and asanas without any thought. It's almost as if we are channeling sacred knowledge of poses from the Akashic record, or another field of knowledge and wisdom. I've assumed yoga poses that I never knew of, but that my partner would recognize from her more extensive daily practice, or we'd find in a partner yoga book.

Engaging in a Tibetan Yab-Yum asana position, where partners hold foreheads together to connect their third eyes, is particularly recommended when the moment feels right.

Additionally, you can create a deeply unified experience with naked dancing to music genres that resonate with both individuals, such as music by "Yaima" that spirals balanced masculine/feminine as well as earth energies. My favorite song of theirs to dance to is "Odonata."

Partner yoga can be another powerful modality to flow energy for yourself and to your lover. Exploring the sensation of slip-sliding over each other's bodies with massage oil can be a magical sensation, too!

Yab-Yum with third eye connect position.

Like MDA, some guys can often be rendered unable to achieve a woody for a good segment of the six- to eight-hour journey, but have no fear, things will rebound. Of course, an MDMA session can be as short as four hours or up to 12 hours if you boost by 25 to 50 mg throughout the day. Keep the total dose to less than 200 mg total, and definitely less than 250, or you will have a longer recovery.

Child's pose with bow posture (heart-opening position for top one).

For gals and guys, achieving orgasm may take longer, but will be much more intense once it's reached. For more creative couples, partners can stimulate a male's G-spot on the prostate along with the penis stimulation to achieve atomic orgasms while awaiting the reboot. Gals, likewise, may need longer, more artful stimulation of analogous regions—including the clitoris and G-spot simultaneously—to reach climax. Take your time, and wait till later in the journey, if needed. Butt play for both can be especially pleasurable with this molecule. Just remember to use plenty of lube!

And remember to exercise caution when using MDMA, particularly for individuals with heart conditions or anxiety. Advanced heart scanning such as the Cleerly scan (https://cleerlyhealth.com) can be performed on psychonauts over 50, offering a high-level screen and hopeful reassurance before using this molecule. Consulting a psychedelic medicine physician and/or specialist is advisable for those with medical or psychiatric conditions that may be exacerbated by MDMA.

Testing the molecule for potential fentanyl contamination using reputable test strips like those sold by "Dance Safe" (https://

dancesafe.org/) is highly recommended. It is crucial to maintain proper hydration and electrolyte balance throughout the experience, so snack on fruits and berries to replenish energy. Coconut water is a great means to hydrate and maintain electrolyte balance. Add a magnesium threonate (Neuromag) supplement (1000 mg) to calm nerves an hour before taking MDMA. Taking 100 mg of grape seed extract and 500 mg of Vitamin C can also be helpful at the start. If you take an SSRI or SNRI, it is best to taper off these prior to doing MDMA under provider guidance. There are also some excellent internet resources available, such as the Psychedelic and Antidepressant Drug Interaction and Tapering Guide by psychiatric pharmacist Ben Malcolm at https://www. spiritpharmacist.com/ADpsychedelicGuide.

Following a journey/roll, I strongly recommend 5-HTP at 100 to 200 mg/day for five days beginning 24 hours after MDMA ingestion, combined with either NAC 500 mg/day and/or Glutathione 1000 mg per day. Oral NMN and/or NAD (IV) can be especially helpful if you are one who struggles with major fatigue post MDMA. Magnesium Threonate mentioned above, taken during and after the journey, can help reduce the edginess of MDMA. If you have an IV therapy center near you, four grams (4000 mg) of Glutathione by IV push can be magical by accelerating one's recovery, too. Try to do this push within a day or two of the journey, and repeat the next day if needed.

Be sure to do your MDMA journey on a day where you have the next day or two to recover before returning to work or a busy schedule. On your recovery days, plan to take it very easy, and don't overdo it physically or mentally. Keep up with hydration, add some extra electrolytes if nausea occurs, and practice mindful-based activities. You may still feel the heart-opening aspects of this molecule for two to three days.

Sometimes you may struggle with depression and irritability after an MDMA. Keeping up with post-journey supplements for a week, engage in mindful-based activities, and avoid making big decisions or attending stressful meetings. Basically, just avoid overstimulating yourself. Those of us over 40 will take longer to rebound, as well as more sensitive individuals.

Deep Thoughts from my MDMA Journeys...

Being open to the energies of this molecule as it opens our field of consciousness, allows us to intuitively find what will help us evolve to stronger, healthier, more awakened human beings. I've been struggling lately with observations of vibrational energy in our society that lacks the love we should be sharing. Perhaps MDMA can be a catalyst for shifting us into enhanced empathy and love. Even if only 1% of us work with this medicine, our enhanced field of love could begin to shift the consciousness of others around us. Ongoing research suggests that psychedelics may permanently rewire us through the expression of genes (epigenetics), promoting empathy, greater connectedness to nature, etc.[10]

From a more global perspective, our world desperately needs this empathogenic "love molecule" just as much as our natural plant medicines. It would be amazing to share this medicine with the rainforest shamans who have an interest. The cross-cultural sharing of medicines should be fostered to nurture ourselves into a global united tribe, not a divided one. I'm witnessing too many people claiming they should control plant medicine based on their cultural roots. If we align with that perspective, one could say that synthetic molecules should be controlled and distributed by modern chemists and pharmacists to only those who are worthy, too. Let's keep them available for all and use them in a safe, respectful, and conscious manner.

Having Indigenous tribes lead the discussions regarding access and use of plant medicines they discovered is sensible and ethical, but we must collectively find ways to foster equitable sharing of these to people of all ethnicities and socioeconomic status for the greatest good. Otherwise, this is just another human game of greed and control, under the false veil of charlatans proclaiming "love and light" to maintain their individual control.

We need guidance from Indigenous elders and shamans who share their plants to make sure they are protected and shared in a sustainable, intended way, while minimizing drama and seeking ways to make it available for anyone that could benefit from its healing properties. Reverend Immanuel Trujillo from the Peyote Way Church of God stated it well- "Peyote is a sacrament for all–no one church, race, or government can own it." I am hopeful that Indigenous elders whose ancestral lineage is with Ayahuasca, Iboga and other plant medicines will share Immanuel's perspective too.

Imagine a roundtable discussion with shamans, Indigenous elders, and conscious psychedelic facilitators enjoying MDMA together as they speak openly from their hearts, not their egos, seeking collaborative solutions. Imagine both parties in Congress doing this, too! Ha, OK, I agree, Congress will need some additional psychedelic therapies to come together and accomplish anything!

I often question our deeper role on this planet. It seems most humans are here to compete and game each other for success and survival, rather than being present in the now, with a heart-centered approach of altruistically loving and helping others, and protecting our planet. MDMA seems to awaken a primal remembrance of how we once were, and how we were as innocent children. Perhaps this molecule and other plant medicines can open our hearts more to love and a sustainable, more altruistic future.

We all have primal roots to draw from, and a "remembering" from past lives that needs to be fostered for our growth. Let's share and make all plant medicines and modern molecules accessible and sustainable for the greater good of the planet. This takes a heart-centered, loving approach that must disregard the color of our skin, our language, sex, orientation, country, or our net worth.

We also need to work more with legislators to help make them more readily affordable and accessible for healing. The medicalization of MDMA and psilocybin has the potential to improve access for many who would not seek it in the underground, but it needs to remain affordable. We have now seen the insane annual costs that Oregon is charging providers to be licensed for psilocybin therapy. This is not sustainable and speaks of governmental greed. Medical practices will have to charge too much to make up for the insane overhead of annual certifications and licenses to provide it in their clinics. In Denver, Colorado the first Psilocybin center just opened in 2025! I'm hopeful that it and many other centers will be successful, sustainable, and affordable to those seeking psychedelic therapy.

A win/win model of continued underground facilitation with logical, affordable access in the medical office setting will provide the greatest good. Many additional practice-based research opportunities will become available in the medical model, but we must also do our best to keep big Pharma from over-capitalizing on psychedelic medicine and limiting access by charging too much.

Over the last decade, we have witnessed numerous unethical 500% or more increases in prices for things like insulin, just because they can. They can because they pay lobbyists to influence Congress, telling them not to pass legislation that would make medication costs more reasonable. Luckily the cost of insulin and a few other meds were recently reined in, but this needs to happen for all medications. On average, Americans pay four times more for the same medication compared to the rest of the world, and many simply can't get their medications due to cost, or insurance not covering them. Some resort to purchasing them in Mexico or Canada if they can afford to travel there.

In regards to psilocybin therapy, most will prefer affordable individual journeys at home, retreats, or in small circles with friends to avoid paying the high cost of a medical office psilocybin session. Having them available in a medical office is important though, as it will allow many who are afraid of trying psilocybin without medical supervision to hopefully become confident enough to venture out into the world of shamanic circles, or enjoy solo work to improve wellbeing.

Let's come together in love and understanding, seeking the greater good for all. Again, by appreciating our varied perspectives and finding common ground with everyone at the table, we can move this psychedelic renaissance forward on many levels! OK, enough philosophy—here is just one of my romantic MDMA stories I'd like to share. I could write a few books on this molecule alone!! Enjoy...

Communing with Mount Shasta with the deep, juicy, love of MDMA!

Mount Shasta

It was late September and Bella and I desired a change of venue beyond Colorado. It had been a couple of years since I'd done a shamanic retreat at Shasta, so I suggested we head there for a heart-opening, nature- and Telos-connecting retreat. Telos is considered to be the "City of Light" connected to ancient Lemuria, which exists inside the mountain. The lost continent of Lemuria was proposed to have existed in the Indian Ocean, per zoologist Philp Sclater in 1864, and then mythically disappeared under the ocean like Atlantis. Many New Age folks feel Lemuria had deep spiritual significance, and was perhaps the ancestral home of early humans. Mysteriously, I've always felt connected to this mountain, especially as I've experienced powerful Kundalini energy flow and visions meditating on Mount Shasta's vortexes.

Offering this exciting adventure to Bella was met with an enthusiastic and resounding, "Yes!"

Since this is also her favorite molecule, we find ourselves journeying with it typically once a month. More than twice monthly is a bit much for us. Everyone varies in their tolerance and calling to this, just like other psychedelics.

Flying into Medford, Oregon, we rented a car and headed south, passing Ashland, then further south towards Shasta. Stopping at the store along the way, we grabbed some food for our retreat, including strawberries, blueberries, and honey for yummy journey treats. Arriving before sunset, we found the cozy cabin we'd booked for three nights. Walking up to it, a sign above this circa 1980's style structure read: "Quan Yin Cabin."

"Ha, love it, perfectly named!" I said. It's conveniently located just a 10-minute walk from Stewart Mineral Hot Springs and a 20-minute or so drive to the base of Mt. Shasta. Nestled amongst a few other cabins, with meditation benches along the trail in a pine forest, and the cascading Parks Creek just below, it's the perfect place for a relaxing nature retreat.

Sleeping well overnight, we were greeted to a blue-bird day. The fall colors of oaks intermixed with ponderosa pine created a diverse color array for the morning sunshine. A couple of small black-tailed deer walked by to say hello during our morning coffee.

After eating a balanced breakfast of scrambled eggs and fruit, we set intentions to go on a journey to enhance love for each other, while simultaneously radiating this field of energy out to all others on the planet and out into the universe.

On the main floor of this beautiful cabin with a loft, we moved the couch back a bit and then laid down two yoga mats, covered them with a large fleece blanket, and placed our pillows and ceremony items adjacent to us. I kindled up a small fire in the wood-burning stove to warm the place up a bit from the cool morning temps.

Starting with our usual 100 mg, we began to feel the flow coming after about an hour. This began the uptick in our heart rates and the subtle feeling of heart opening and root chakra opening. As the slight edginess of the first dose lightened after an hour, we took another 50 mg of MDMA along with a light 1000 mg (one gram) of psilocybin. Soon we found ourselves deep in the empathogenic flow of MDMA. We kissed, and held one another, holding our hearts together.

Before long, we desired some music and movement. Pulling up my heart medicine playlist, it began with some music by RUFUS DU SOL. Singing the "Innerbloom" song together, "If ya want me, if ya need me, I'm yours!"

We ecstatically danced without any inhibitions, embracing and kissing one another in perfect flow. Time disappeared, bringing presence and awareness to one another, carefree of the world around us. Deep eye gazing, followed by playfulness and frequent laughing, helped us let go of our stressful week.

Heading outside to the deck with a Bluetooth speaker, we danced with the towering lodgepole pines surrounding us, the sound of the cascading stream below us, and Mount Shasta in the distance. Feeling the cool breeze and the pines surrounding us with their feather-like branches spiraling to the sky, engaged us in a more primal, yet sensuous flow. It's as if a tribe of trees were holding space for us as we danced. The light mountain breeze teased our hair, infused us with the refreshing smell of the pines, and added the shimmering sound of aspens around us. Nature was our facilitator, and the medicine allowed their carbon-based love to flow into us as we danced. Ecstasy in nature with my partner is quite different from a rave.

After a good hour of dancing, we brought our yoga mats and blankets to the deck. We rested for a while, holding hands and watching the clouds drift by in the deep blue sky above. Observing clouds shaped like dragons, unicorns, and more was all we needed. Having the urge for more movement, Bella motivated me to do some partner yoga with her. She's a daily yoga gal, compared to my once a week practice, so I let her lead me through several poses. Nothing too challenging, but poses included; Temple, DoubleTree, Double Boat, Standing Forward Fold, Supported BackBend, and my favorite, Flying Superman! We finished it up with some individual poses, too, all aimed at opening our hearts and flowing prana from root to crown in a more amplified way with the medicine.

Child pose with root chakra activation.

Shavasana/Child's Pose.

As it became cool outside, we decided to head inside and lay out the blankets again in front of the wood-burning stove. Feeding the fire with some small oak logs, to further enhance the ambiance, we lit a few palo santo candles around us and grabbed some bowls of fruit we'd left in the fridge.

Laying down, we deeply embraced each other, interlaced our legs together, and relaxed into the field and magic of simply "being."

After a good while of holding each other, Bella rolled over and asked me to gently massage her breasts. I positioned myself on my knees, sitting gently over her upper pelvis, and stared into her sweet brown eyes. The flame from the fireplace behind her reflected in her pupils. How perfect.

Looking into her eyes, I said, "You're so beautiful babe, it's so hard to express with words the deep love I feel for you now, but I'm going to simply flow love from my hands into your body in a way that hopefully captures what I feel towards you."

I held my right hand out, cupping the lower part of her left breast, feeling her heart.

"Bella, please hold your right hand to my heart, and let's gaze deeply into each other's eyes."

Doing so, we both felt the most profound primal, energetic connection ever. Holding this for a good 10 minutes, we experienced tears of joy rolling down our cheeks, followed by another embrace.

Soon I honored her original request and squirted some warmed massage oil onto my hands, then gently circled the oil on her perfectly rounded breasts with my fingertips. Taking one hand, I flowed an infinity (figure 8) pattern between her breasts. Closing my eyes allowed me to feel the prana flowing to her heart chakra and breasts more intuitively.

"OMG, this feels amazing, Astraeus," she said, "I feel like letting go into you."

Applying more lavender-scented almond oil, I began to do a deeper circular massage on both breasts and then spoked it out around her chest.

"Don't stop!" she said. "I've never felt your hands with so much love!" Looking at her sexy body glistening from the fire was so arousing. I leaned over to lightly kiss her breasts.

"Ooo, love that," said Bella.

Massaging her upper chest, I worked my way up to her neck and then repositioned myself with her head face-up in my lap. Massaging the back of her neck, her head, and then her jaw/ TMJ felt amazing to her as I relieved some of the muscle tension related to the effects of MDMA. Using the tip of my right index finger, I flowed rainbow light into the region of her third eye between her brow. She jolted slightly, feeling the energetic flow from my fingertip, which I spiraled down to her root chakra and yoni. I reached for her heart and left breast to send more energy there and held this pose for a good five minutes.

"Whoa, it's crazy how I can feel this flow more from you while on the MDMA," she said.

"I know, I can feel it flow more intensely from me to you, too! I'm just bringing the energy in from the stars above, through my crown, down my arm, through my fingertip, and into your third eye," I shared. "This molecule increases the bandwidth and strength of flow similar to shifting from a coax (cable) to fiber optic connection."

Taking a break from tantric massage and energy flow, I reached for the strawberry, placed it in my mouth, and then shared it with her. She did the same for me, followed by some sips of cool coconut water, and deep passionate kisses.

Holding each other in Yab/Yum asana, we connected our third eyes again.

She desired some body work on her back, so she laid back down as I began to flow energy from her root to her crown with massage along her spine, and some energy work. Sitting just below her ass, I could feel her root chakra resonating so much energy towards mine. The MDMA and her flow lit my root chakra on fire with an intense sensation! The medicine was flowing through me too intensely to make love to her at this point.

Moving her legs apart a bit to sit between them, I began to do some deep tissue work on her beautiful butt. Loving the circular flow with the base of my hands, followed by even deeper work with my elbows, I then followed it with some gentle massage between her cheeks. Dripping more warm oil between her butt cheeks, I gently massaged the region intuitively with my fingers. As I gently teased her anus with a well-oiled fingertip, she began to moan more. Slowly, she started to move the energy in her pelvis, lifting up, and then making some sensuous circular motions. Closing my eyes again, I let my energy flow while I felt her gently swirling her hips, facilitating the flow more deeply.

Shifting focus, I began massaging her thighs and calves, followed by gliding them down to her feet and toes, flowing even more love.

"OMG Astraeus, this may be better than the last tantric massage you gave me. How can they keep getting better and better?"

"I think this medicine lights up our sensory neural tracts allowing us to flow our prana (qi) more readily every time, baby," I said.

"Mmm love it, your geeky energy talk is arousing, baby," said Bella.

"Bella, I sooo want to go down on you. Is that cool?"

"Of course, baby!"

Rolling her over on her back, I ascended towards her yoni, and very gently kissed her.

"Whoa, I'm so crazy sensitive right now!"

"I can tell!" I said.

Gently circling her clitoris with my tongue, she moaned. As I teased her for a timeless period, she said, "You've been tantrically torturing me forever now!"

We both laughed, and I went back down on her. I rolled her over for a bit to kiss her sweet ass, and to run my tongue between her cheeks for some erotic butt play. Flipping her back over again, I went back down on her clit while slowly stroking her G-spot with a finger. She felt herself on the verge of coming for what felt like 20 minutes or longer as she moaned continuously in an ecstatic state. Feeling my tongue near exhaustion, she suddenly released with some of the greatest intensity and duration I'd ever witnessed her do!

"OMFG, Astraeus, that was an insanely powerful orgasm. Hold me and breathe with me."

Laying in a space of timeless oneness together, we embraced in a state of ecstasy.

Some moments later, she sat up and said, "It's time for me to torture you now, baby!"

"Ok, bring it on baby, I trust you."

Laying down and looking up towards the ceiling, Bella sat down on my lower pelvis, looking towards me with her sculpted breasts accentuated by the flickering fire behind me. She asked me to exhale deeply, then placed her mouth on mine, sealing her lips to mine, and gently filled my lungs with her breath. The warmth of her breath flowing into my lungs combined with the prana expressed by her was so intimate and loving. I breathed this love back into her, followed by some deep passionate kisses.

She massaged my face and chest in a caressing tantric manner, followed by working her way down to the root chakra. Grabbing our favorite large Tibetan bowl, she then positioned herself with her legs on top of mine and feet towards my face, so that her butt touched mine.

The Tibetan bowl was then placed to simultaneously resonate her yoni and my complementary parts. Chiming the side of it with the rubber mallet resonated the healing vibration into both of our root chakras.

"Astraeus, I love how this activates my Kundalini energy! Do you feel this, too?"

"OMG, yes, keep it going!" I said.

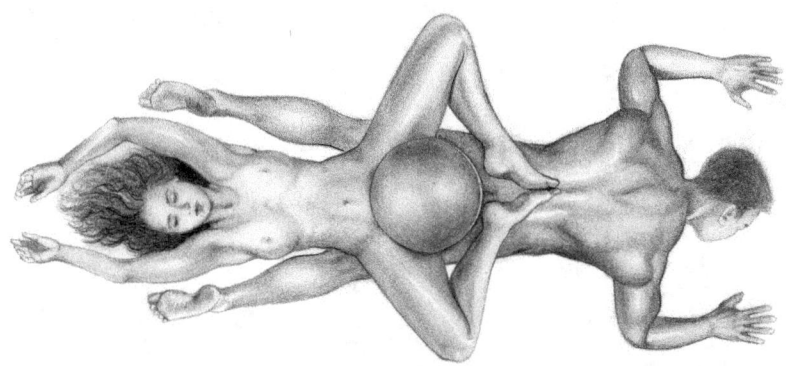

Resonating our root chakras chiming a Tibetan bowl.

After another 10 minutes or more of bowl-chiming, Kundalini stimulation together, Bella sat up and spun the bowl for a more continuous flow of this sacred geometric sound into me.

"I want you to do this on my lower spine, babe."

Rolling me over, she spun the bowl another five minutes, flowing more vibrational energy into my root. She then worked the muscles in my neck, back, legs, and feet with her magical healing hands as I felt myself melting more into the floor. Lubricating my back and buttocks more with massage oil, she glided her perineum up and down my back, and then to my neck.

"Whoa, this feels so good, rubbing my yoni up and down your spine!" she said. "Especially on the prominence of your sacrum, Astraeus."

"Mmm loving that, too, and I can distinctly feel a flow of intense energy emanating from your yoni into my back. Keep going as long as you'd like, baby." She continued, as I obliged to be her slippery-slide pony!

"Mmm," I said, "let's remember the slippery-slide pony play for the future, babe."

"Astraeus, I love how this medicine allows us to do these wild things with each other without any hesitation or judgment of one another."

"Me, too."

"How about we do some partner yoga and flow our energies even more? I'd love to do a forward flying pose," said Bella.

"Sounds great!"

She positioned me on my back with a yoga mat underneath, then I aligned my feet on either hip.

"Extending my legs fully, I lifted her up as she balanced her upper body, holding my hands. Once we stabilized the pose, she extended her arms out like an eagle, expanding her heart chakra. Letting her fly with this pose and the MDMA, we took deep cleansing breaths and could feel expansive heart energies flowing between us. *So powerful and beautiful*, I thought.

I wish I could push a video record button and capture this, but simply being in a balanced flow in the now was our goal. After a few minutes, my legs began to fatigue and I let her down slowly. Didn't want a crash landing! She positioned herself into a child's pose, and I laid back with my back on hers. This offered deep grounding for her after her flight. Soon we did the same poses with her lifting me into the flying pose. Her well-toned quads and core strength lifted me with ease as I struggled to maintain the perfect balance she manifested. Showing off a bit, she pumped me up and down a few times with her sexy thighs. Soon I arched my back, extended my arms, and found myself flying like an eagle too! After another round of child poses with her lying on my back, we positioned ourselves to hold one another deeply, savoring the moment.

Forward Flying Pose.

"Astraeus, let's do our scissor legs and feel our root chakras connecting."

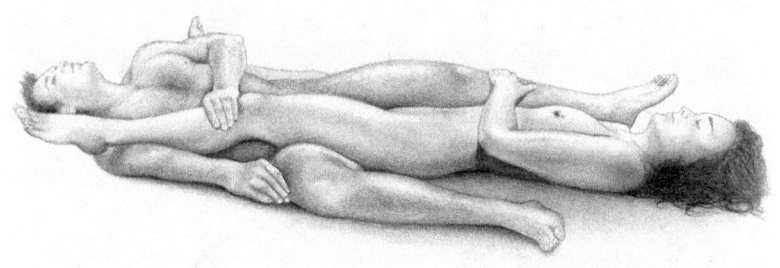

Root chakra spiraling via perineums in our scissor position.

Positioning myself with her as our feet aimed towards each other's heads, then holding our hands, we pulled our perineums in tightly to each other.

"Whoa, so much energy flowing here now. Let's spiral our Kundalini energy into each other feeling this ball of fiery energy flow up our spines and out of our crown chakras. I love how the yoga poses earlier amplified this for us," I said.

We held this position for a while, feeling our energies ignited down here even more. We now call this amazing position the "root lock".

"I want to kiss you between your legs," she said.

"Mmm, I'd love that, Bella." Running her tongue down my chest and down south, she tortured me with the most amazing oral sex.

"OMFG, I'm so crazy sensitive right now!"

"Ha! Now you know how I was feeling when you went down on me, too!" she said.

Soon I was hard and aching, as she alternated between slow and fast, then stopping and gently teasing the tip of my glans with her tongue.

"Mmmm this is so amazing, I keep feeling like I'm on a continuous verge of cumming, Bella. My root chakra has never felt so activated."

She continued to torture me for what seemed like forever.

"OMG, I want to release, but the MDMA is keeping me at 99% there. This continuous verge of orgasm feels amazing, but it seems if I don't release, I'll go crazy!"

"Don't worry, babe," she said, "I'm going to help you along and tease your G-spot."

Lubing up her middle finger, she slowly entered and began a gentle circular motion at the center of my prostate. Applying a little more pressure, and alternating with some back and forth, I could feel myself coming so much closer to orgasm. As she went faster with her mouth on my cock while also increasing the intensity, circular speed, and pressure on my prostate, I finally let go with one of the most intense and prolonged climaxes ever. The intense orgasm spiraled like a bolt of lightning up my spine and blasted out of my crown chakra with a wildly ecstatic expansion of my energy body. Bella paused to let me breathe while keeping her finger motionless inside me.

"I feel like you've expanded my aura beyond where I've ever gone, baby!" I said.

I thought, *G-spot orgasm on MDMA, the final frontier, where few men will go*, as I reminisced on Star Trek's Captain Kirk saying, "Space the final frontier... to boldly go where no man has gone before."

"Wow! Thank you for such a magical and powerful release, Bella."

Breathing deeply and slowly, I embraced and hugged her several times, as we felt ourselves merging into one. The oxytocin between us must have been sky-high. We napped for a while by the fire before grabbing a light dinner and heading to bed.

"You know, Bella, I want everyone on the planet to experience this level of merging love, oneness, ecstasy. To die without experiencing this level of ecstasy is a shame. Imagine how much better everyone would get along if we could all experience what we did tonight. Maybe I'll start by writing a book and perhaps this will shed awareness and allow others to experience these higher, more profound levels of love."

"Yes!" she said. "You must share how others can experience this ecstatic interdimensional love, Astraeus."

"I'll start writing when we get home. I have the book in my heart and will share it soon. Thanks for being on this wild planet with me, babe." Later that night as the MDMA faded, we made love a few more times, before passing out in complete exhaustion.

The next day, we hiked some of our favorite trails on Mount Shasta, including Panther Meadows. I found a vortex area I wanted to show her from a visit years ago. Arriving in the area, I used a dowsing rod to localize the vortex.

Positioning ourselves in half-lotus, we meditated, facing one another for an hour. Feeling the presence, energy, and love of Telos below us, we entered a space of oneness and deep love of Mother Gaia. Honoring the mountain, the archangels, and the spirits of the mountain, we decided to make a lemurian medicine wheel. Holding each crystal to our hearts, then to our third eyes, we breathed our love and intentions of healing the planet into each crystal. Digging down several inches into the dirt, we first placed the large central Lemurian crystal pointing to the sky, followed by orienting and placing selenite wands with smaller Lemurian points in the four directions. Blessing the wheel after sharing healing prayers for Gaia and the ancestors of the land, we sprinkled tobacco, and then buried the wheel for eternity.

Mount Shasta Crystal and Selenite Medicine Wheel.

On our final day, we relaxed and decompressed further in the Stewart Mineral Hot Springs, followed by some ice-cold plunges in the creek before noon. Feeling somewhat fatigued from the journey, we nourished ourselves with a long nap, more 5-HTP, NAC, and time holding each other wrapped in blankets, sitting on the deck. What a magical weekend!

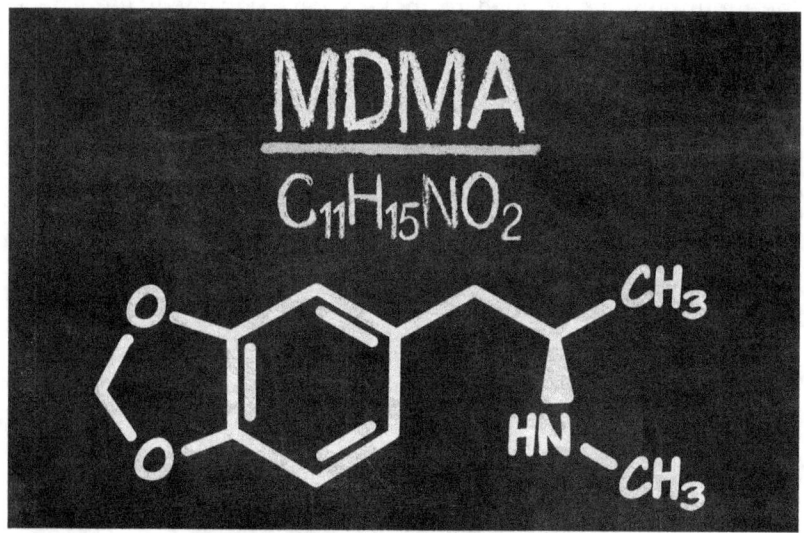

MDMA Summary

How It Works

- Phenethylamine psychedelic, serotonergic amphetamine, 3,4-methylenedioxymethamphetamine.

- Release of monoamine neurotransmitters: Serotonin > Norepinephrine and Dopamine.

- Binds and stimulates serotonin 2A receptors.

- Neuropeptide release of oxytocin and vasopressin (ADH).

Metabolism of MDMA

- Complex hepatic metabolism via multiple CYP enzymes CYP2D6 (major), CYP2B6, CYP3A4, CYP2C19, CYP1A2.

- Converted to active (MDA) or potentially neurotoxic metabolites (HHMA, HMMA)

- Auto-inhibitor of CYP2D6.

- CYP2D6 poor metabolizers may have higher concentrations of MDMA.

- Duration of journey, about three to six hours, possibly longer if booster dose is used.

Typical Dosing

- Typical doses are moderate and begin with 75 to 125 mg by mouth, followed by booster dose equal to 50% of initial dose (37.5-62.5mg) 90 to 150 minutes later.

- Clinical studies show that the use of MDMA in three sessions spaced about one month apart has increased benefits.

Common Journey Experiences

- Fear reduction and empathogenic heart opening.

- Deep unconditional love for your partner, those in circle and oftentimes love to the greater world around you.

- Major increase in tactile sensation or sensitivity to touch.

- Improved communication to your partner (opening of throat chakra).

Potential Therapeutic Uses

- Treatment refractory Post-Traumatic Stress Disorder (PTSD).

- Alcohol Use Disorder.

- Social Anxiety in autistic adults.

- Depression and Anxiety associated with life-threatening illness.

- Couples therapy.

Potential Adverse Effects

Physical

Nausea
Lowered appetite
Fatigue
Increased blood pressure & heart rate
Seizures**
Serotonin Toxicity**

Psych/Neuro

Emotional discomfort
Anxiety
Low mood & irritability (post-journey)
Insomnia
Poor cognition*
Addiction**

*Commonly reported after use.

**Associated with high doses, overdoses, unsafe drug combinations, or recreational use.

Potential Drug Interactions & Contraindications

- SSRI/SNRI → Muted effects & reduced efficacy.

- MAOIs → Contraindicated, Serotonin Toxicity.

- Lithium → Contraindicated, increased risk of seizures.

- Benzodiazepines → Possible reduced efficacy.

- Stimulants → Increased risk of stimulant toxicity.

- Ritonavir/cobacistat → Serotonin Toxicity.

- CYP2D6 Inhibitors → Increases blood concentrations of MDMA.

- Other CYP (CYP1A2, CYP2C19, CYP2B6, or CYP3A4) Inhibitors → May increase blood concentrations of MDMA.

Legality

MDMA is regulated as illicit or Schedule I substances by the United States federal government, although has been given a "breakthrough designation" by the Food and Drug Administration (FDA) due to its potential as a treatment of PTSD. The FDA has also granted an expanded access program to allow persons to receive the investigational drug ahead of approval. https://maps.org/mdma/ptsd/expanded-access/

Australia made headlines in 2023 as it became the first country to allow prescription access to MDMA. It is expected MDMA assisted therapy will be FDA approved in 2024. https://www.nature.com/articles/d41586-023-02093-8

Chapter 6

San Pedro and Peyote: Mescaline Medicines of the Andes and Southwest

Huachuma (San Pedro, *Echinopsis pachanoi*) is an entheogenic cacti with properties that profoundly connect you to nature, Pachamama (Mother Earth), and your lover through its heart opening and root chakra activation. The primary psychoactive alkaloid mescaline is a phenethylamine, thus it shares structural overlap with substances like MDMA and works to promote an increase in dopamine, norepinephrine, and serotonin levels, as well as binding 5HT2A receptors directly. However, mescaline is fairly distinct from MDMA in its subjective experience due to the extensive duration of action (MDMA ~four hours while mescaline ~12-18 hours). 2-CB is also a phenethylamine, but with much greater heart opening effects and a shorter duration compared to mescaline.

These properties engender heightened tactile sensations, gentle euphoria, an intense flow of Kundalini energy, and visionary experiences that unveil vibrant auras, intricate geometric patterns, and vivid colors in plants. I strongly recommend being in nature with this cacti, given its ability to link you deeply into surrounding plants and trees.

Huachuma (San Pedro) Cactus.

The sacred journey of Huachuma is classically embraced for 14 hours, with the final four hours being particularly conducive to sacred sexual experiences. It is recommended to embark on this journey mid-morning, allowing ample time to immerse oneself in nature, and engage in activities such as hiking, yoga, and meditation. As the sun sets, the enchantment reaches its peak, and the intimate act of making love becomes a transcendent and magical culmination. This cactus, affectionately referred to as Grandfather, holds a lineage dating back 10,000 years to the Andes. Huachuma thrives in the wild, predominantly gracing the western slopes of the Andes in Ecuador and Peru, flourishing at altitudes ranging from 5,000 to 10,000 feet. Additionally, many individuals cultivate Huachuma sustainably for its ornamental and medicinal purposes. Initially employed in ancient rituals by the Chavin civilization, it was later adopted and cultivated by the Quechua natives and continues to be used ceremonially by Huachumero shamans.

During the early years of Spanish colonization, the Roman Catholic Church discovered that this sacred cactus facilitated a connection with higher consciousness via Saint Peter. Hence it was named "San Pedro," since Christians believe he holds the "key to the heavens" and perhaps it gave humans a glimpse of it. In a process known as syncretism, missionaries would blend local religious traditions with Christian symbolism, and nomenclature to make Christianity more acceptable to the native populations.

However, despite honoring Huachuma with the name San Pedro for religious conversion purposes, the church ultimately feared them having a direct connection to the divine by drinking this tea, leading to suppressed access and removal of Huachuma as much as possible.

This columnar cactus can be prepared into a tea by someone experienced in the procedure. It can then be consumed fresh or dehydrated into a powder that is effective as well. The amount of tea or powder to consume should be guided by a facilitator or instructions specific to the product. As with other plant medicines, it is best to become familiar with it in a shamanic circle before doing it with your partner in a sacred sexual container.

If you are not lucky enough to have the tea prepared, the extremely bitter powder is best mixed with apple juice, stirred thoroughly, and consumed rapidly. A battery-powered wand or a Ninja blender is useful to dissolve the powder. Let it sit for a good hour. Some are now making Huachuma chocolate bars, and more purified mescaline from the cactus, making it an even easier way to go! Be sure to consult the maker of these products on safe dosing, as it will vary based on the concentrations they prepare.

A Journey to the Land of Enchantment

Bella and I love making trips down to Santa Fe, New Mexico, to check out the diverse selection of art on Canyon Road, the historical buildings, the southwestern vibe, and amazing restaurants. Spring and Fall are prime times to visit. Making the trip down in late April, we spent a couple of days enjoying the sights and flavors of historic Santa Fe, followed by a short drive north to one of my favorite hot springs in the country, Ojo Caliente! Booking one of the casitas with an adobe fireplace and private tub next to the sandstone cliffs is always best for a romantic escape.

After some dinner and a late evening soak, we enjoyed some intimate time before passing out and sleeping deeply through the night. On this trip, I decided to also pack some dried Huachuma, day hiking gear, and some quartz crystals. I wanted to experience the land and the springs in a more interdimensional manner with my lover, going beyond the 3-D.

In the morning, we awoke to a beautiful crisp spring day, with deep blue skies and wispy clouds above. After a light breakfast, we both agreed it would be a perfect day for a Huachuma adventure!

Packing our lunch, snacks, and plenty of water in our daypacks, we looked over at a Ziplock full of Huachuma.

"Mmm, this won't be like your morning vanilla latte, babe," I said, "but I think you'll enjoy the perks a lot more!!"

We placed several grams of the dark green powder in a half liter of apple juice for each of us and thoroughly mixed it. Drinking the bitter brew slowly, and then chugging it, we eventually managed to get it all down.

"Bella, this is the one time I'd actually enjoy a Krispy Kreme donut to balance this bitterness!" I said.

Lacing up our boots, we smeared ourselves with sunscreen, and with hats on and packs on, headed out to the trailhead. The BLM trail behind the springs has some amazing loops, or "out and backs." We decided to take one of my favorite loops that's a few miles long. Heading up the dusty trail, we found this April day to be warmer than most. Easily in the mid-70's at 9 AM. Cactus and juniper covered most of this rugged, dry, terrain, and the geology had a mix of red sandstone, limestone, scattered quartz, and jasper.

As we approached the top of the ridge, rolling rugged maroon-colored hills could be seen in the distance, with some gentler ones just down the trail a half mile or so. One small hill curiously caught my eye.

"Bella, let's take that small trail up to the top of the hill. I'm being called to check it out."

She smiled back, acknowledging that enigmatic phrase I often use. Walking along a primitive trail that seemed more like a game trail, we came to the peak of the hill, which was relatively flat. White quartz crystal was everywhere! Interesting, as we hadn't seen an outcropping of quartz anywhere in the region till we arrived on the hilltop.

"Whoah, I must have been pulled in by the energy of this place!" I said to Bella.

"That feels so true," she said.

"Check it out, someone has created several large rock cairns over there."

Walking over, we could see six large pyramid-like piles of white quartz that others had made.

"So beautiful to see that others have been tapping into the field of energy here and amplifying it by making these cairns," I said. I pulled out a blanket and laid it amongst the crystal cairns.

"How about we meditate and feel into this energetic field more together, Bella?"

"I'd love that, Astraeus!" Sitting half-lotus, with our backs touching each other, we did a silent meditation with deep, slow breaths.

After about 45 minutes, we began to feel the plant medicine coming on.

"Are ya feeling Grandfather Huachuma?"

"For sure, feeling a little ungrounded right now though, babe."

"Me, too."

I turned around to hold her from behind and we guided ourselves through more slow breaths while feeling our root chakra connect more intimately to Pachamama.

"Feel ourselves connecting to the water table below," I said. "Let's go deep into the earth, just like the juniper trees surrounding us."

Doing so, the intensity of our crown chakras was balanced more as we took in the aura of the trees around us. We began to see a visible field of energy (auric field) emanating from the juniper branches, and a flowering prickly pear cactus.

"So amazing how I feel one with nature dropping in with this plant medicine, Bella. Other psychedelics do this, too, but this takes the depth of it up a couple notches, easily."

"Agree," she said.

"OK, let's stop talking and just drop in, babe."

She was right; sometimes I talk too much and need to simply be. So blessed and grateful to have her with me on all these journeys, and for her redirecting me as needed. While I have done plenty of solo journeys, having my partner or a friend with me has always amplified the experience.

We silently meditated, letting go of our monkey minds and default mode networks, and tapped into nature. We felt a light breeze, smelled the rich scent of juniper, and listened to the gentle, higher-pitched frequencies of the wind as it glided through the trees.

We both began to feel more root chakra activation and amplified Kundalini energy. Holding her hands, I could feel the energy radiating and connecting more profoundly through our central palms. Still holding her from behind, I placed my right hand over her heart, and my left index finger to her third eye region. I spiraled my cosmic energy through my left hand, and heart-centered love through my right hand, flowing it down to her root chakra, and then deep into Pachamama. Breathing deeply and expanding our auras as one, I felt like we were making love to Gaia.

"Bella, I feel so grateful for you, and even more grateful that you and I can spiral our love and energy into Mother Earth as we are right now. This takes 'earthing' to another level. Let's send our energy all the way to the core of Pachamama now, feeling the energies of Pele' as we share our love with her."

"Loving this, Astraeus, I want to feel your hands around my lower Dantian."

I placed my left hand a few fingers' breadth below her navel, with my right hand on top to help flow more yin energy. We continued to meditate and be present amongst this vortex of energy we'd discovered.

Quick sidebar—While I don't practice Qi Gong regularly, I did take a year-long course a decade ago and still enjoy a few poses. The Dantian is considered to hold the centers of vital energy, known as Qi or Chi, that circulate throughout the body. I often refer to energy centers interchangeably via the Traditional Chinese Medicine perspectives or Tantra (Ancient India healing tradition). The lower Dan Tian is in the region of the Tantric Sacral Chakra (Swadhisthana), near the second chakra, typically two inches below the navel.

Chakras with the lower Dan Tien in the region of Second Chakra (just below the navel).

The Kundalini stimulation from the San Pedro had kicked in within an hour or so, and we could both feel it needed to be grounded. Looking around, I could see an arroyo (desert wash) just down the hill from us.

"Bella, let's head down to the arroyo for some deeper grounding."

"Awesome idea; I see some trees we can hug down there, too," she said.

Leaving our crystal hilltop vortex, we hiked down to the dry, sandy, bed of the arroyo.

"Wow, check this out, Bella, the sand is crazy saturated with large granular white quartz!"

Partner Kundalini Flow.

Sliding off our hiking boots, we sunk our feet and then our hands deep into the sand. Immediately we both felt an energetic release into the grounding nature of the sand and arroyo.

"OMFG, this release and grounding feels soo healing, babe."

"I feel it, too," Bella said. "Holy cow, try this downward dog position with me!"

By doing so, we felt an even more potent connection with the land. We then sat down with our backs together and legs spread apart, holding hands and allowing ourselves to ground out into the cool sand together. Soon we could feel the Kundalini energy grounding out a bit, taking the edge off the intensity of this San Pedro.

Later we were called to commune with a beautiful pinon pine adjacent to us. On opposite sides of the tree, we pressed our third eye onto the bark and embraced the loving energy of this tree together. Feeling so much more balanced after this arboreal flow, we decided to resume our interdimensional trek.

Hiking along the trail, the rocks took on a new level of attraction. The jasper and quartz looked like appetizing treats, and I felt like reaching down to eat one! Every natural thing felt 10 times more sexy to me. The blooming cacti flowers popped vibrant colors like never before, and the radiance of the leaves seemed otherworldly.

We walked slowly and in synchrony with nature. Looking down, my boots would frequently morph into moccasins. After a couple of miles, we came upon a historical ancient Puebloan ruin. Not much remains, other than faint traces of foundations, and geometric black and white pottery shards, as one might see at Mesa Verde.

I envisioned the families living off this harsh landscape. Difficult as it may have been to forage for wild game and plants, they were blessed with the mineral-rich natural hot springs below for drinking and healing soaks.

I can't imagine how deeply the Native Americans connected to this enigmatic land in New Mexico. The mescaline flowing through my veins gave me some glimpses of it, but I so desired some kind of time machine to authentically witness this place. Walking respectfully and not taking any artifacts, we felt as if spirits of the land were hiking with us, and holding a container of sacred energy with us.

"Bella, do you feel an ancient loving presence right now?"

"Yes, for sure, Astraeus."

"I'd like to place a crystal here to honor these people. Are you feeling that, too?"

"Of course, I'm so in flow with this," she said.

Reaching into my day pack, I pulled out a quartz seed crystal. Holding it to my heart, then to hers, we blessed it, dug a small hole adjacent to some sagebrush, and planted it to honor these people and the land. Feeling the essence of heart opening, we knew this was embraced by the spirits around us.

Leaving the site, we headed to the edge of the ridge where we could see the small creek flowing downstream from the hot springs area.

The sunset was coming soon, so we scouted a nice flat area and laid out a blanket to take in the evening colors. Watching the shadows of vibrant green junipers elongate on multi-hued distant rolling hills, reminded me of Georgia O'Keefe paintings. Bella held me from behind as we were mesmerized by the changing colors. I could see why Georgia eventually settled at Ghost Ranch to live and paint, just up the road from this spot.

Huachuma can last 14 hours or longer, so we were still deeply activated by it. Taking in the unique southwestern tones of a New Mexico fiery sunset is something to be experienced, and repeated again and again.

Twilight arrived, so we packed up our things and descended the trail with headlamps to our casita. Entering the room felt surreal after being in nature all day.

"Let's go outside under the stars and relax in the Kiva hot spring pool, babe."

"Sounds perfect," she said. Slipping into our swimsuits, we headed to the Kiva hot spring a short distance from our room. Amazingly, we had it to ourselves!

We alternated supporting each other gently as we floated weightlessly on our backs and looked up at the stars. We enjoyed such a deep sense of oneness with the universe, and a loving connection to Gaia, as we were embraced by her thermal waters, warmed by igneous flow deep below us. Holding our breaths, we submerged ourselves and sat half-lotus together a few times.

"I'm loving this embryonic feeling from these healing waters, Astraeus!"

"Me too, babe."

Closing my eyes in this dimly lit pool, I was happily surprised to see a significant amount of geometry and color.

"Close your eyes, Bella. Are you seeing lots of geometry, too?"

"Yes, so nice to see that Huachuma is still with us!" We sat timelessly, eyes closed, taking in the geometry and color, alternating with viewing the beautiful stars above. After a while, we decided to head back to the room.

Walking into the dark room and flipping on the lights was intense, so I lit a few candles and kindled a fire in the small adobe fireplace, then turned the lights off.

"OMG, I so desire to be naked with you, Bella. Being in nature was amazing, but let's simply be one again now."

Watching her slide off her bikini top, and seeing the beautiful contours of her breasts and nipples was so arousing. She slowly slid off her bottom, exposing her cute ass.

"Come and get me, baby!" she said.

Sliding off my wet trunks and finding myself so hard at this point, I hopped in bed and kissed her passionately. Closing my eyes, the kaleidoscopic imagery began to amplify as I kissed her followed by us gently touching our third eyes together.

Holding back on the urge to fuck her immediately, I descended on her breasts, kissing them, making them wet, and then blowing on them gently.

"Mmm, love it when you gently tease my breasts, baby."

Soon I began to alternate with some gentle bites to her nipples, followed by taking a generous part into my mouth, then back to gentle.

"Astaeus, you're making me so wet and aroused that I can hardly stand it. I want you inside me soon. Also, my sensitivity is so heightened with this plant medicine."

"Hang in there, I want to slowly savor you and drive you to where you can't stand it anymore, Bella."

"OK, but I'll call uncle when I can't stand more of this slow torture."

Working my way down to her navel, I tickled it with my tongue in a circular pattern. Soon I dropped down to her yoni.

"OMG, you are crazy wet, babe!" I said. As I slowly teased her with my tongue, she moaned and began to move her hips with almost every movement of my tongue.

"OMG babe, I'm ready to cum already!"

As she released on my face, I could see a complex and beautiful lotus flower before my closed eyes. The lotus flower changed colors and then seemed to have an opening centrally representing a portal. Not saying anything, I gently placed my third eye region on her yoni and sensed myself going through it, then opening up into an expanded universe of geometry. *Wow,* I thought. I seem to be traveling inter-dimensionally through her yoni! I would have never expected something as astral as this during oral sex!

"Babe, I just experienced a portal you created. It's too much to share now, but let's integrate this later for sure."

Ha, who knew Bella was a walking portal!?

"Astraeus, I want you inside me now!"

Coming up for air, I smiled and asked, "Are you sure?"

"Not funny, I'm getting on top of you now!"

Rolling me over, she positioned herself on top with the most determined, fiery look in her eyes. Gazing deeply into my eyes with her sweet breasts dangling elegantly above me, she came down slowly on my aching cock. The energy of her wet yoni spiraled wildly as she slowly made love to me. At this point, I thought I might instantly explode in her, but somehow managed to avoid that volcanic moment. Continuing to slowly torture me, she picked up the tempo, then stopped with me deep inside her as she gazed again into my eyes. Closing my eyes, and simply being present for her magic,

I felt myself merging into her again.

She leaned down to briefly kiss me, then went back to riding me. This time much harder, faster, and deeper. Placing my hands on her hips, she began to do me with such wild intensity.

"Love it when you dominate me like this, Bella!" I could feel her back getting sweaty, and her hair and breasts now bounced ecstatically above me. She began to moan and rolled her eyes up towards the ceiling.

"I'm getting so close!"

"Me too, baby! Let's spiral ourselves into oneness now, and explode into the universe above us."

Soon, the fractal imagery and color increased, and I could feel our root chakras up to our crown merging. Feeling the intense pressure in my root chakra, we both spontaneously climaxed.

Cumming for what seemed like eternity, I felt an explosion of our unified divine masculine and feminine out into the universe. Holding her breasts as I stayed inside her, we experienced one of the most profound, sustained, ecstatic states ever. Thanking the universe, gods, archangels, and interdimensional fields of light, for everything that manifested today, including the "magic yoni portal". We laid down exhausted, holding each other in divine bliss.

Peyote

This small, cute, but powerful spineless cactus (Lophophora williamsii) is native to the deserts of Mexico and the Southwestern United States. It has been used for thousands of years in healing and religious ceremonies by the Indigenous groups, most notably the Huichol of Mexico, and Native American Tribes, particularly the Navajo, Apache, Comanche, Kiowa, Ute, and Lakota. They use it legally within the Native American Church (NAC).

Peyote Cactus.

Peyote buttons are harvested by carefully cutting the above-ground part of the cacti from the root. Harvesting of this sacred, psychoactive button is done with respect and often involves specific rituals and prayers.

Dirt is cleaned off each button and sometimes the small "tuft" of hairs (the cactus's vestigial leaves) is removed from the center of the button.

The buttons may be eaten as is, ground up to eat, dried for use later, or boiled to make tea. The consumption of Peyote is typically done in a ceremonial context with specific rituals and under the guidance of a knowledgeable leader, often referred to as a Roadman or Roadwoman in the Native American Church or a shaman in other Indigenous cultures. The ceremony involves prayers, chanting, and other ritual elements that are integral to the experience and are meant to facilitate a spiritual journey or quest.

Peyote use within the NAC is legal for members of federally recognized tribes in the United States due to the American Indian Religious Freedom Act Amendments of 1994. This law provides a legal exemption for the use of Peyote in traditional religious ceremonies. However, outside these specific legal and traditional contexts, Peyote is classified as a Schedule I substance in the United States and is illegal to possess, use, or distribute.

A bit of history. The use of Peyote spread north to Native American tribes during the late 19th and early 20th centuries, leading to the foundation of the Native American Church, which integrates Peyote rituals with certain Christian beliefs.

Conservation concerns arose recently due to increased demand for Peyote, both for religious use and illegal trade, combined with habitat destruction as it is foraged. This has led to concerns about the plant's sustainability, which is protected by various American Indian Religious Freedom Acts as well as by Proposition 122 in Colorado. Efforts are ongoing nationwide to ensure sustainable cultivation and harvest.

Visionary Perspective of a Peyote Ceremony.

So how does it work?

The primary psychoactive compound in Peyote is mescaline (3,4,5-trimethoxyphenethylamine). It's a phenethylamine, which means its structure is somewhat related to neurotransmitters like dopamine and norepinephrine.

Mescaline exerts its effects primarily by binding to serotonin receptors in the brain, particularly the 5-HT2A receptor. This binding alters the typical patterns of serotonin transmission, leading to alterations in mood, perception, and cognition.

Psychoactive effects of mescaline include visual and auditory hallucinations, altered perception of time and space, euphoria, introspection, and, in some cases, anxiety or agitation. The Peyote experience is often described as profoundly spiritual or insightful, and it can vary significantly among individuals and contexts.

In terms of safety, mescaline (Peyote & Huachuma) is generally considered to have a low potential for addiction and is not known to cause physical harm when used responsibly. It can, however, be intense and psychologically challenging for some. Potential interactions with other substances or pre-existing mental health conditions can complicate its effects. Besides mescaline, Peyote contains other alkaloids, albeit in smaller quantities, which might modulate the plant's overall psychoactive effect.

As with many traditional substances, the use and significance of Peyote go beyond its pharmacological effects. Its role in cultural, spiritual, and historical contexts is profound and warrants respect and understanding.

A few years ago, I was invited to be in a circle with a Native American Road woman who was willing to occasionally include outsiders. I felt blessed and honored to be in this circle. After following her dieta, I arrived to be in a circle with ten others. The Peyote buttons were ground up and mixed into water in a thick paste and other ritual foods were placed following her Ute tribe traditions. Passing the talking stick around the circle, we each shared intentions/prayers, followed by a fairly long series of additional rituals by the Road woman. Soon after we consumed the Peyote, we were blessed with her singing beautiful traditional songs.

I found this medicine to bring in many visuals and introspective insights for me. The colors and geometry were beautiful and more subtle than those I've experienced with the Ayahuasca ceremony. The healing potential feels similar for both plants. Having the opportunity and honor of experiencing this medicine that grows close to where I live, and embodying the profound healing energies of a Native American holding space is something I will never forget and will cherish.

In summary, Peyote has offered profound inward healing to me in a sacred circle. Because of its sacredness, I feel this plant medicine should be experienced in a Native American facilitated circle, whereas San Pedro can be experienced in a shamanic circle or a sacred ritual container with your lover. I hope that someday, Peyote will be shared and available more broadly to help so many in need of its healing potential. Like other plant medicines, some are beginning to propagate and grow Peyote sustainably, hopefully leading to greater availability in the future. Most importantly, I hope that Native Americans can continue to offer it to their own tribes, maintaining the sacred tradition and training of generations of roadmen and women to come.

Once the Indigenous healers can expand out to others more, it could serve as an opportunity to heal the wounds of the past. As they help others gain a deeper understanding of Native American culture and their traumas through this plant medicine, I hope to see greater compassion and reciprocity from outsiders to help them, and to protect Turtle Island (North America).

Insights I've received from these plants and the Roadwoman have included:

- Caring more for the planet, all inhabitants, and our environment.

- How to become a better father and partner.

- Understanding my spiritual self and my energy body on a much deeper level. Even seeing my chakras and meridians in out-of-body journeys on these plants.

- Letting go of the fear of death.

- Letting go of my ego.

- Visualizing how to share love with the universe.

- Flowing into oneness and dissolving cultural barriers.

- Greater compassion and understanding of others, especially those from different cultures.

- Enhanced heart-centeredness, allowing me to provide deeper love for my partner and enhanced sacred sexual flow.

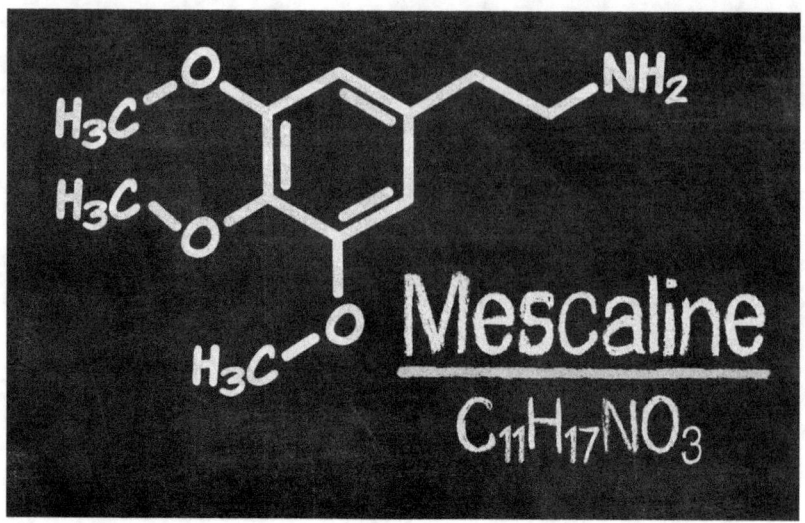

Mescaline Summary

(The psychoactive component in Peyote & San Pedro)

How It Works

- Classic phenethylamine psychedelic, 3,4,5-trimethoxyphenethylamine.

- Release of monoamine neurotransmitters: Serotonin > Norepinephrine and Dopamine.

- Binds and stimulates serotonin 2A receptors.

Metabolism of Mescaline

- Unclear metabolic enzymes, likely undergoes hepatic metabolism due to O-demethylation (CYP2D6?) and amine oxidation (MAO?) are two predominant metabolic schemes, although mescaline can also be eliminated unchanged.

Typical Dosing

Dosing of Mescaline

- Threshold: 100 mg

- Light: 100 to 200 mg

- Moderate: 200 to 300 mg

- Strong: 300 to 700 mg

- Different salt forms of mescaline have different molecular weights, making dosing strengths somewhat dependent on salt form used (HCl vs. Sulfate).

- Relative to other psychedelics, mescaline has low potency.

Dosing of Mescaline Containing Plants

- Mescaline is commonly dosed in dried Peyote (lophophora williamsii) buttons or in a prepared beverage or dehydrated power from San Pedro (trichocereus or echinopsis pachanoii, as well as related cactus species). Note that Peyote is an endangered species and official sacrament of the Native American Church.

Common Journey Experiences

- Fear reduction and empathogenic heart opening.

- Less intensive effects than MDMA or psilocybin over a much longer duration of time

- "Peakless" psychedelic with onset of effects in ~one hour, peak effects from ~three to eight hours, and comedown phase from ~eight to14 hours.

- Single episodes of emesis during hours one to three is relatively common.

Potential Therapeutic Uses

- Anthropologic records suggest that ritual Peyote use can help Native Americans suffering from alcohol use disorder, however, there have been no modern-day clinical research trials using mescaline for any therapeutic indication. This may be due to the prolonged duration of action, limiting suitability for psychedelic-assisted psychotherapy applications.

Potential Adverse Effects

Physical

Nausea; One-time emesis possible
Decreased appetite
Increased blood pressure & heart rate

Psych/Neuro

Emotional discomfort
Anxiety
Insomnia

Potential Drug Interactions & Contraindications

There has been very little biomedical research performed regarding drug interactions and mescaline. The following are predicted from known drug interaction potential with MDMA and/or psilocybin. It may be reasonable to extrapolate from these molecules due to their metabolic, structural, and pharmacologic overlap.

- SSRI/SNRI → Muted effects & reduced efficacy.

- MAOIs → Contraindicated, Serotonin Toxicity.

- Lithium → Contraindicated, Increased risk of seizures.

- Benzodiazepines → Possible reduced efficacy.

- Stimulants → Increased risk of stimulant toxicity.

- CYP2D6 Inhibitors? → Increases blood concentrations of mescaline.

Legality

Check the specific laws and regulations in your state and local area to determine the current legal status of San Pedro and Peyote (Mescaline).

- It is illegal to possess, distribute, or use mescaline under federal law.

- Some states have specific laws regulating the possession, sale, or use of mescaline-containing cacti.

- Some states have made it legal to possess San Pedro cactus for ornamental or horticultural purposes.

- Local ordinances can also impact the legality of San Pedro cactus.

2-CB

An amazing synthetic relative of mescaline and MDMA, known as 2-CB is a molecule everyone should experience. This molecule, in my opinion, is one of the top three for sacred sexuality. I hope all psychonauts are lucky enough to find a safe source for this molecule and enjoy it at some point!

2-CB (4-bromo-2,5-dimethoxyphenethylamine) is a synthetic psychoactive substance that belongs to the class of phenethylamines. Discovered by Alexander Shulgin in 1974, he referred to it as one of the "magical half dozen." This list includes mescaline and other members of the 2C family, such as 2C-E, 2C-T-2, and 2C-T-7.

I was unable to find a source for this amazing molecule until 2 years ago, and now, after a good 25 journeys with it, I feel that I can share the experience in this latest edition.

Shulgin told the Center for Cognitive Liberty and Ethics: "**2C-B is, in my opinion, one of the most graceful, erotic, sensual, introspective compounds I have ever invented.** For most people, it is a short-lived and comfortable psychedelic, with neither toxic side-effects nor next-day hangover." 2C-B was popular in the club scene in the 80s and 90s. In 1995, it was classified as a Schedule I substance in the U.S., like MDMA. (Please be aware of legal implications with this one, too.) It's considered to be both a psychedelic and an entactogen due to its effects on perception, mood, and consciousness.

I and others consider the experience to feel somewhat like a blend of LSD and MDMA. At smaller doses of 10-12mg, the psychedelic effects are light, but the heart opening remains profound. At 25mg and higher, the psychedelic effects become more notable.

The specific action of 2-CB on the brain is not fully understood, but it's believed to primarily affect serotonin receptors. Acting as a partial agonist at serotonin 5-HT2A and 5-HT2C receptors, it also affects dopamine receptors, although to a lesser extent. This may contribute to its mild stimulant-like effects and the rise in libido and passion that is encountered with this molecule. The duration is typically four hours but can last up to six hours. We usually feel the effects around 75 minutes, and it peaks at roughly 2 hours.

The experience varies widely among individuals, but commonly, one may experience light visual geometric patterns, enhanced sensory perception, mood enhancement, increased empathy, heart-opening, and passionate love towards one another..

Nausea may occur at doses over 15mg. Taking Zofran (Odansetron) Rx or natural ginger 15 minutes prior to taking this molecule can help mitigate this. 2-CB is less "rampy" than MDMA, with a lower likelihood of feeling jittery as well.

Like MDMA, partners will feel deep levels of connectedness and a desire to hold, caress, and to flow energy tantrically to one another. You'll feel roughly a 7/10 MDMA level of desiring to hug your lover, so if you want to amplify it a bit, MDMA can be added in at a low dose.

Dancing to music, followed by sensual body work for psychedelic sacred sexual foreplay, allows one to smoothly drop in together, as you allow your rising kundalini energy to amplify.

As you dance, consider holding your third eyes together. Later, if it calls to you, apply some massage oil or cream and slide up and down your lover's back with your perineum in a flowing "slippy-slide" fashion (mentioned in the MDMA chapter) to wildly ignite your senses for each other. No judgment of each other. Just flow and be. Don't be shy and ask your lover what you or your partner desire. Hot stone massages, followed by placing hot stones on your lover and laying on top of his or her body, heightens the experience even more.

Savor the developing flow of rising sexual energy and let your intuitive energy-body awareness guide you further. As you begin to connect more deeply, more passionate kisses, with a desire for oral sex, or giving each other some love bites may follow. Take your time, no agenda, and no need to rush into lovemaking.

Unlike MDMA, achieving orgasm is typically easier—unless you're exploring higher doses, where the intensity may initially make lovemaking more challenging. Be patient, surrender to the experience, and allow the connection to unfold naturally. When orgasms do arise, they tend to be profoundly intense, often prolonged, and for women, can be multiple and transcendent. Guys can have transcendent ones too, and both of you may see an enhancement of color and geometry and sometimes even portals as you release with your eyes closed. Don't forget to journal your sensual experience and integrate what came in for both of you the following day.

The "Nexus Flip"

After you've experienced several journeys together with 2-CB, you may want to try combining low-dose MDMA with it. This is called the "Nexus flip". Typically, taking 50-75mg of MDMA 30-60 minutes prior to taking a 10-15mg dose of 2-CB works well. Others advocate waiting for 2 hours before taking the 2-CB, but we've found the overlap enhances the loving connection more. You'll need to do some R&D on what works best for you with combinations. Just remember to always start low dose. Neuromag

500-1000mg is also recommended along with a nausea medication (Zofran) or supplement (ie ginger), since it will be a bit more intense. Alternatively, sound healing by spining or chiming a Tibetan healing bowl in the upper abdominal region, third chakra can work well.

A booster of 5mg of 2-CB can be done after 2-3 hours if desired to increase the empathogenic flow in a journey of 2-CB alone or in combo with MDMA. Remember to follow a post-roll protocol if MDMA was used.

Following the journey, 30-60mg of CBD tincture or a light dose (2mg) of Indica THC gummy can help you fall asleep if needed.

2-CB/THC Flip

Bella and I have found through our personal Love Shack R&D lab that 12-15mg of 2-CB combined with 2mg of Sativa THC and 2mg of Indica THC via rapid release via edible gummies is another amazing combination. This further enhances psychedelic imagery, erotic flow, and sensations. Orgasm potentials are increased for both of us, and believe it or not, Bella has had over 25 orgasms in an evening with this combination!! While I could never achieve that number, the intensity of 2-3 profound O's is more than enough for me with this molecule.

While 2C-B is generally considered to have a manageable safety profile, like any psychedelic substance, it should be used with caution. It is not without risks, and high doses or combination with other substances can lead to adverse effects. Testing with a Dance Safe test strip to rule out fentanyl contamination is recommended on each new batch.

Going deep in the Carribean!

Bella and I decided it was time to reconnect with the ocean blue this spring. We both enjoy scuba diving and sailing, and after some online research, we decided to book a trip to Turks and Caicos. I'd dived on many of the other islands in the Caribbean, so I was excited to explore a new island. This series of islands is lined with beautiful white sand beaches, turquoise waters, and scenic walls of reef to dive. The windy side has great conditions for kite boarding and wing-foiling.

Turks & Caicos were inhabited by Taino and Lucayan Indians for at least 700 years before Columbus arrived in 1492. They lived peacefully and were skilled in farming, fishing, and gardening. However, when Columbus arrived in 1492, the Lucayan civilization began to disappear, and the islands soon became sparsely populated. Later, the salt-making industry was born, drawing Bermudians to Turks & Caicos to rake the salt and take it back to Bermuda.

In 1962, Turks & Caicos became a British Crown colony and began to develop into a posh tourist destination. Well, enough history, let's get wet!

After a magical week diving the vibrant reefs in the depths of the Northwest Wall of Providenciales and West Caicos and racing across turquoise seas on a Hobie Cat with steady wind in our sails, we realized it was time to slow down and dive deeper into the realms of sacred sexuality. Amidst the beauty of this island paradise, we were tapping into the intimate love that mirrors the ocean's own mystery and depth.

Earlier in the morning, we placed three lemurian crystals in coral reef crevices with the intention of helping them sustain growth and to protect them from the threats of climate change. Coming back to our relatively isolated Airbnb, we set intentions for ourselves and for more global healing of Gaia. Holding 50mg of MDMA with 2-CB to our hearts, we gently took them down with a few sips of cool coconut water.

Strolling along the shoreline as the sun melted into the horizon, we gave the molecules time to awaken within us. With each barefoot step in the warm sand and each breath of salty ocean air, we deepened our connection to the earth, the water, and each other.

As we began to feel our root and heart chakras being positively attenuated, we decided to head back to our beachside retreat. If the beach was private, we would have entertained the idea of getting naked and wild on a few towels, but the no-see-ems bugs are another challenge on his island!

Making it back, we headed to the bedroom and began to dance to some Porangui tunes. Slow erotic dancing ensued, and we found ourselves slowly disrobing each other, dancing naked within minutes. Feeling the enhanced sensation of our skin, her nipples rubbing across my chest felt magical. I reached behind her squeezing her sweet ass tightly, feeling the primalness of the medicine kicking in. Pulling her tight to me, I could feel my cock throbbing and wet against her yoni. Continuing to dance, with a spiraling motion in our hips, we gently kissed and embraced.

Descending slowly to her navel with her standing, I then flowed my tongue down on her yoni. Giving her a few gentle licks between her legs, her hips began to quiver. Making a little shuffle to the cool wall she braced her ass firmly against it allowing me to tease her more wildly circling her clitoris with my tongue. "Omg baby, you are insanely wet!" I said. "Wow, you're seriously dripping down your legs, but I love that!" I began to alternate with tongue circles and gentle sucking on her clit as I remained kneeling on the floor.

Soon, she began to breathe more deeply, and her moaning increased. Gently stimulating her G-spot with a come-hither motion with a fingertip, I could feel her approaching climax. Her vaginal walls and G-spot began wildly contracting, followed by a screaming orgasm. "Babe, you just squirted on my tongue!" Unable to talk, she continued to moan, followed by another orgasm. Several more intense ones followed as I gently teased her more with my tongue. Eventually, she cried uncle, and I stood up to give her deep, passionate kisses.

"Babe, I want you to fuck me now!" said Bella. Lifting her while against the wall, she wrapped her legs around my hips, and I entered her fiery, hot, wet yoni. Thrusting slow and deep, then faster with the wall bracing us, my feet grounded into the floor as we made vertical love. Spiralling the energy from Gaia up through our feet, to our hearts, and then out our crowns as we made love felt primal and ecstatic. The heart-expanding and root chakra intertwining energy of this molecule and our love amplified the sensations for both of us. Within ten minutes, we both came together wildly, then stumbled to the bed, collapsing to catch our breaths and cool off momentarily.

Laying down, we embraced one another, placing our 3rd eyes together and feeling an amazing tingling flow between us. As our hearts went even deeper together, we shared how much we loved each other with an immense feeling of bliss and oneness laying there.

The intensity of the molecules was building as we were close to 2 hours, and I felt the need to be grounded by some energy work.

"Bella, can you do some tantric massage and energy work to help ground me out?" "Of course, babe," she said.

Grabbing her special organic/orgasmic massage cream, she began to work my neck and shoulders, followed by an amazing low-back and ass massage. "Bella, please sit on my lower spine to help me ground even more." Doing so, I could feel her yoni rubbing against my lower spine. "That feels so amazing. Grease me up with some cream down there and slide your yoni up and down my root chakra and lower spine area, please." As she did this, I could feel my entire energy body relax and melt into her.

Soon, I felt myself doing the same for her. Moving and balancing energy, allowing the medicine to intuitively show me where to go with my hands and body with Bella. Periodically, we'd pick up on stuck or unwanted energy that needed to be extracted and balanced in each other. Once we finished this, we moved on to more fun together.

Soon, our sexual desires began to rise again, leading us towards a little foreplay.

"Bella, I want to caress your G-spot as you use your clit toy". Firing up her toy, she applied the little suction cup on her clit, as I gently stroked her G-spot. Within minutes I could feel her vaginal walls contracting and another wild orgasm manifesting for her. Plateauing for what seemed like an eternity, I slowed my g-spot stimulation and simply applied medium pressure, feeling her contract and come again and again.

"Astraeus, I want to be on top of you now," said Bella. Rolling over for her, she positioned herself on top, facing towards my feet. I love it when she's assertive in bed. Slowly, Bella descended her yoni on my throbbing cock teasing me with short descents, followed by deeper ones. Sensations were so enhanced for us that we could feel every cell resonating with each slow glide into each other. The campfire of energy was being stoked to a bonfire. Soon, she began to ride me faster and faster. Holding her hips, and watching her beautiful ass bouncing down with grace, I could feel the intensity of an orgasm building for us.

Taking longer than usual to cum with this molecule, we slowed the tempo for a while, feeling and flowing our kundalini in a more artful enigmatic dance as she squeezed and shifted her pelvis subtly. Soon, we returned to a more deep and intense primal mode. "Fuck me harder Bella!" I said. "Oh yes, I will!" she said.

Feeling like we were both on the edge of climaxing for ten minutes, we finally released together with ecstatic screams. Holding her with me inside her for another few minutes, we savored the after-burner energy flow of such amazing orgasms.

Laying back down, listening to Yaima on one of our playlists, we drifted into bliss, feeling energetically expanded into the depths of the universe. The cool air gently blowing down from the AC with a light breeze from the slightly opened window felt amazing on our sweaty, salty bodies.

Desiring to drop into a more psychedelic state towards the end of our 2-CB, we reached for a fast-acting Indica gummy and split one between the two of us.

Soon, organic patterns manifested visually with eyes closed, further highlighted by a flickering candle on the bedside table. Observing the patterns as they morphed from the synesthesia of hand-pan music, we eventually fell asleep into an astral dream world...

Chapter 7

LSD: Flowing Multidimensionally into Nature with Your Lover

LSD (lysergic acid diethylamide or "acid") is the most potent psychedelic, thanks to its profound activity in the microgram range (a standard hit of LSD is 100 ug or 1/10th of a single mg!). Personally, I feel it's in the top three for psychedelic sexuality. Yes, you'll just need some stamina to enjoy the prolonged benefits of this one and will need to relax the next day, but it's all worth it!

This molecule is renowned for its long-lasting nature and wild reputation thanks to Woodstock and its impact on visionary art and the music world. It may carry a higher degree of stigma relative to other psychedelics, due to the somewhat uncontrolled use during the 1960s hippie movement.

This remarkable substance was discovered by Albert Hoffman at the Sandoz laboratory in Switzerland. Interestingly, it was initially set aside for five years before Hoffman accidentally absorbed 250 mcg of it, leading to the infamous "Bicycle Day" on April 19th, 1943. Many of us continue to celebrate this momentous day in April! But please don't go out and ride a bike on it.

Today, LSD is commonly used in neurobiological research relating to psychedelic mechanisms of action, yet so far has not been tested in as many clinical studies involving persons with illness relative to MDMA or psilocybin. An interesting recent discovery was that LSD (beyond binding 5HT receptors) can directly bind tyrosine kinase receptors that are directly linked with stimulation of neurotrophic factor expression such as "Brain-Derived Neurotrophic Factor" (BDNF). This molecule has incredible promise in unlocking new avenues for mental health treatment, although may still be hampered by its past reputation or have such a lengthy duration of action that it is less preferable for therapy sessions.[11]

From the psychedelic community perspective, I've witnessed this molecule being held in a more sacred container compared to the past. Many apply its remarkable magic towards spiritual awakening while immersed in nature, deep visionary work, artistic stimulation, and sacred sexuality.

Since LSD can profoundly impact one's sensual and visual experiences, it's a favorite choice among psychonauts seeking high levels of sacred sexual flow. It's also an amazing modern shamanic tool for visionary work. For most, it enhances sexual activation (libido), particularly by lighting up your root chakra, but by also hugely enhancing sensitivity to erogenous zones and your entire body. However, the intensity of this effect can vary from person to person with some experiencing a less pronounced impact.

The activation of both 5HT2A and D2 receptors by LSD contributes to the heart opening and heightened sensation. It can create a unique environment where lovers may feel a shamanic connection, allowing them to metaphorically shape-shift into otherworldly beings. During an LSD journey, auras can become visible, and the perception of geometry and colors can become incredibly vivid and intense. Geometric grids often become visible on the ground, and at higher doses, the patterns can be seen in the sky, descending and connecting to trees and plants below.

If you are new to LSD, starting with a dose of 50 to 100 mcg is generally recommended. Due to the eight to twelve-hour duration of the experience, I recommend starting early to mid-morning and immersing yourself in nature, if possible. Finding a secluded spot in the woods with a blanket can create a serene setting. If inclined, consider alchemizing the experience by bringing along some crystals, a musical instrument, sacred geometric forms, or other items that are called to join you on this experience. Alternatively, you can connect your favorite mindful music playlist to a Bluetooth speaker or earbuds. Of course, if you have the opportunity to be near a mountain stream, waterfall, or the ocean, simply tap into nature to complement the journey. Don't forget to pack plenty of water and snacks, with bug repellent and sunscreen on hand if needed.

A steamy, tropical adventure!

Costa Rica has been one of my favorite places to explore for decades now. Their dedication to preserving and preventing further rainforest deforestation compared to other countries with tropical forests is to be admired and hopefully adopted to prevent the loss of species and accelerated climate change. While they can't prevent all deforestation, they currently have preserved 28% of their land in their parks and wildlife refuges and benefit from roughly $4 billion in eco-tourism income annually.

Back in the 80s, I had an incredible opportunity to partake in a month-long undergraduate rainforest ecology and botany class, which helped further amplify my intimate connection with nature.

Exploring the diverse rainforest biomes and immersing ourselves in the enchanting flora and fauna has made me a life-long advocate for wilderness preservation. I vividly remember the incredible opportunity I once had to photograph the elusive golden toad in its natural habitat at Monteverde Cloud Forest preserve, a memory that brings sadness as this magnificent species has regrettably gone extinct. However, amidst the melancholy of losing one beautiful creature, I find solace and hope knowing that I can still witness the existence of my all-time favorite exotic bird, the quetzal, still thriving gracefully in the enchanting cloud forests. This enigmatic flying feathered serpent was revered by the Maya as a symbol of their god, Quetzalcoatl.

The golden toad's disappearance serves as a poignant reminder of the delicate balance of nature and the urgent need for conservation efforts to protect our planet's biodiversity.

As I embark on my journeys to visit forests and coral reefs, I am reminded of the responsibility we all share in safeguarding the world's natural wonders. Observing the vibrant plumage and graceful flight of the quetzal and other endangered species, I am reinvigorated to contribute in any way I can to ensure the survival of these fragile creatures and the preservation of their habitats for generations to come.

My walks in forests continue to be more of a mindful meditation, especially when I walk barefoot, earthing myself like the roots of a tree, and observing subtle elements such as the spiraling patterns of branches in a tree, or the species and patterns of mushrooms on the forest floor. I'm not that guy trail running in spandex with a water bottle bouncing off my butt, yelling at people, "On your left!" Life is too short to dodge the intimate details of a forest ecosystem.

Why digress on this topic? As mentioned earlier, research has shown that psychedelics may increase "nature-relatedness,"[12,13,14,15] and in my case, I'll confirm that it's done that and more through an even deeper, more intimate knowing and love of nature.

So perhaps more people tripping out on plant or synthetic psychedelics may lean towards a collective consciousness of nature conservation. Pair a psychedelic journey with an immersion in nature, and you'll soon find yourself hugging and talking to the trees around you!

This past spring, I suggested to Bella that we explore one of my favorite regions of Costa Rica. She was excited to explore this country, since she hadn't been there yet. We desired to keep it simple and explore one area on this trip and decided to head to the Volcan Arenal region. Flying into San Jose, we overnighted, then rented a car to drive the windy roads to our destination.

Stopping at lush green tropical waterfalls along the way, we walked along the trails to get close to the misty spray, and the dense growth of mosses and ferns. The sound of the waterfalls and the smell of the vegetation were relaxing and grounding. Dodging an occasional stray dog on the road, we passed by coffee plantations, farms, and quaint small towns, eventually arriving at my favorite hot springs resort in the late afternoon. "Just wait, Bella, you're going to fall in love with this place!"

Heading over to dinner by the springs, we enjoyed some seafood and made a short walk to scout out the hot spring pools for the following day's psychedelic journey in nature. That evening, we enjoyed some tantric massage and lovemaking, followed by some deep restful sleep. After a yummy breakfast, I placed a couple of small LSD blotter papers on the table.

"Let's set some intentions before we begin our day with this amazing molecule, Bella."

"Sounds good, my intention is to experience energetic and physical healing, immersing myself in the mineral-rich hot springs, and connecting even more deeply with nature and you, Astraeus."

"Mmm, love that, Aho," I said. "I'd like to embrace your healing and nature intentions too, connect with you more, and also find more self-love. I tend to be critical of myself and need to do a better job of letting go of that. For me to heal myself, and to help heal others, I need to be in a state of unconditional self-love, regardless of my shortcomings of being human."

"Love that, Astraeus. I've been waiting for you to set that final intention."

We placed the small square paper under our tongues, donned our swimsuits and robes, and headed down the trail to the hot springs.

The Tabacon River flows over and is heated by thermal hot springs below, creating a perfect temperature with many of the pools at 100 to 102 degrees Fahrenheit. The nearby active Arenal volcano is part of this geothermal territory, and can often be seen spewing bright red cinders at night from the property. The Tabacon resort is likely one of the most beautiful tropical forest hot springs on the planet. Iceland, Turkey, and other countries have beautiful and unique ones, too, so it's premature for me to pick a favorite until I find time to explore them all!

Entering the springs area, we wandered up the trail to the more private area called Shangri La. The molecule was just beginning to kick in for us, facilitating an enhanced color saturation and natural sacred geometric appreciation. Tall heliconia torch gingers were blooming all over the place, along with orchids slowing us down to a crawling speed as we stopped frequently to take in the beauty and sweet fragrance of the flowers. Large tropical hummingbirds flew around us, dipping their tongues in their juicy nectar, and numerous species of butterflies enjoyed the gardens as well.

Eventually, we made it up to the private area and found a bamboo pod with cushions, providing a perfect setting for our psychedelic nest. Leaving our snacks and water bottles there, we headed to the river, which contained a large hot spring pool. At this point, we were about an hour into the LSD journey, seeing more visuals and feeling the physical sensations more profoundly. The prana expressed from these mineral hot springs of Gaia surrounded us in a nurturing and embryonic manner. Dropping into the gently flowing hot springs in the river, our stimulated nervous system grinned as we submerged ourselves with only our heads above the healing water.

A gay couple just downstream from us smiled as we embraced and held each other. They seemed to politely acknowledge that we were tapping into a different dimension! I thought, *I wish I had some extra LSD for them, too.* Smiling at them and sitting back under a small waterfall, we began to drop in more deeply into the field of nature surrounding us. Placing our heads under the waterfall, our scalps were caressed by the dancing waters, taking us into a more intimate space with nature.

The waterfall began to show more iridescent rainbow light, entraining me into a trance-like state. Soon Bella and I positioned our shoulders under another gentle natural waterfall massager, holding hands.

"Babe, I couldn't ask for more than this right now. This is truly paradise found being with you, in nature, and in psychedelic flow. Let's just simply be in the now and one with all of this."

She simply nodded with a deep smile, acknowledging my thoughts. We now entered a timeless space of ecstasy in nature. I was feeling so much root chakra activation and so wanted to make love to her in the hot spring. *Hmm,* I thought, *too many people around, and I'll just save that energy for later.* At various times, we intuitively wandered into different pools, and waterfalls, experiencing different temperatures, waterfalls, and flora around us. Most of the visitors seemed to be in a mindful state, and if they were being loud or talking about sports, we simply moved to a different pool.

Soon, we went back to our pod and enjoyed some fresh fruit and shrimp for lunch. After a while, we headed down to the spa to get a long massage for each of us. The healing hands of two beautiful Tico gals helped loosen up our muscles and balance our energy bodies even more. We floated into a timeless space together, listening to the cascading river next to us.

Following this amazing bodywork, we headed back to enjoy more of the hot spring pools in the river.

"Bella, I'd love to place a Lemurian seed crystal in the forest back there, and one in this small stream above the waterfall."

"Mmm, I love that idea, Astraeus!"

Finding the two clear quartz crystals in my pack, we dipped back into the pool with both in my hands. Holding them to my heart, I blessed the crystals and said, "We place these crystals to help heal Mother Gaia, and to help send a field of love to all in the world, and the universe surrounding us."

After connecting them to my third eye, I then handed them to Bella to hold to her heart and third eye.

"I want to embrace your prayer, but let's also connect to the light of these crystals, and the grid of crystals around the world that it interfaces with," said Bella. She handed them back to me, and I walked into the forest to place one under a small palm tree, burying it shallowly in the forest dirt.

Following this placement, I made another placement as I inserted it securely under a large boulder in the stream above the waterfall. Swimming back over to her, we both visualized the crystals radiating healing energy into the stream and the land around us.

"Bella, I always feel that the positive energy of a crystal placed in a river flows downstream, helping to heal the land and people it touches."

"That's interesting, Astraeus. I've never contemplated that, but it feels so true."

"So it is, it is done," I said as we completed the placements. We headed back to our pod, ordered a light dinner and drinks from the waiter, and relaxed, gazing into the canopy of the rainforest trees around us.

Heading back to our room, we walked amongst a lush trail with bromeliads, orchids, and birds of paradise. Tree frogs were beginning their dusk-time chirping, and we spotted one enjoying a small pool of water in the center of a tank bromeliad.

Arriving back in the room felt somewhat surreal after leaving the tropical forest. The cool air from the AC was welcomed, though. Peeling off our swimsuits in no time, we hopped on the large bed and quickly embraced each other.

"OMG Bella, I've been dying to feel your naked body next to mine all day!"

"This feels amazing, Astraeus, hold me tighter."

Holding her tight, I could feel her heart beating against my chest. Hugging one another as deeply as we could a few times, I lightly kissed her lips, followed by some deep passionate kisses. Placing our foreheads together, we could feel our third eyes pulsing and spiraling energy back and forth.

"Whoa, so much energy flowing here again, babe, you're zapping me and I'm seeing enhanced circular geometry with my eyes closed!"

Kissing her forehead, then running my tongue around her ears, followed by wet kisses on her neck, I descended to kiss her breasts.

"Babe, you have the most beautiful and perfect breasts!"

Circling my tongue around them broadly, then narrowly, felt amazing for both of us. I reached over for a small jar of honey I'd picked up at a roadside fruit stand and dripped a spoonful on each one. Watching the honey drip down them with rainbow-like colors from the LSD enhancement was otherworldly.

"Babe, I love that cool feeling of the honey dripping down my breasts. I want you to lick it off so slowly, and send me your deepest love as you do it."

Staring at the divine feminine beauty of her breasts, she probably wondered if I was still on the planet. Somehow, I registered her loving request slowly and timelessly and licked off the honey. Gentle love bites, then kisses to her nipples followed as I circled the base of her breasts.

"Astraeus, this is heavenly, keep going!"

After a timeless moment, I put some honey in my mouth, kissed her, and gently pushed a small pool of honey off my tongue into hers.

"So yummy, babe, I want to eat you!" she said.

"OMG, I feel the same towards you, too."

Grabbing a piece of mango on the bedside table, I placed it in my mouth, then let her bite off half as I met her open mouth. Staring deep into her eyes, we savored the taste of the honey and mango.

"I love that it has so much more depth of taste to it than it normally would," I said.

Repeating this a few more times, I decided to dip the chunks of mango in the honey jar.

"I feel like I could do this for eternity," I shared. This upped the pleasure and I slowly squirted more of it into her mouth from mine. This orgasmic-tasting tropical blend hightened our erotic state to another level.

"Bella, I want to kiss all of your sweet, sexy body now." Holding the honey jar over her, I tilted it to allow a golden stream to flow a line from her heart to her yoni.

"Whoa, Astraeus, I can't wait for what's next!"

Slowly running my tongue around her chest and breasts, my tongue then circled down to her third chakra (solar plexus region). Gentle kisses and love bites followed to her belly, followed by more kisses to her navel and dan tien region. Feeling my root chakra on fire, I so wanted to make love to her. Holding off on that desire, I refocused on slowly torturing her with a gentle touch, and savoring her sweet essence.

Making my way to her yoni, I began to circle tease it with the tip of my tongue.

"OMG, I feel like I may orgasm in seconds," said Bella. I held back for a moment, letting her breathe, then more gently kissed her, bringing her to the verge again.

"You know you're driving me insane again, Astraeus!!" As she rocked her hips up towards my face, I went down on her passionately, as she screamed and orgasmed wildly on my face. She breathed through the explosive orgasm, then asked me to go down on her again.

"So, loving this Bella," I said. "I want to make you cum a few more times."

Within a short period of time, she screamed and climaxed four more times.

"Uncle, honey! Let me catch my breath, and I want you inside of me," she said.

"Mmm, I'd love that, babe."

"I want you to make love to me from behind," said Bella.

Positioning myself, I slowly entered her yoni from behind. "OMG Bella, I forgot how sensitive LSD makes me. It makes me feel like I could release in you right now." Restraining myself by tightening my PC muscle, I gave myself more time to feel the amazing energy of her surrounding me as we slowly made love. Taking some deep breaths, I paused a few times deep inside her to allow our energies to spiral into each other and pulse through our bodies. The heightened sensitivity of LSD along with the root chakra activation is so intense that one often has to slow down, allow the energy to flow, and then resume at a tolerable pace.

As the intensity backed off with our slower pace, we began to pick it up again. Holding her sexy butt tightly, we could feel our root chakras on fire as we climbed towards an explosive climax together. Releasing with ecstatic wild screams, I embraced her from behind, still inside her, savoring the post-orgasmic flow. Catching our breath, we then collapsed onto the bed in a state of bliss. Rolling over, we let the cool air bathe our hot, sweaty, naked bodies. After cooling down, we embraced in blissful ecstasy.

The evening continued till 2 AM with more creative love-making positions, oral sex, and multiple orgasms for both of us. We feared a call or a knock on the door by hotel management, but luckily that never came.

As with all of our LSD journeys, we've found this molecule makes us more aroused and multi-orgasmic than any other psychedelic. For myself and other guys I've spoken to, having six orgasms, sometimes even more, is possible with the profound activation and sensations provided by this molecule. Of course, for women, many more. Dosing, molecular purity, set, and setting play a role as well, and I so hope you can find that sweet spot!

We returned the next morning to the hot springs, allowing the waters to rejuvenate our tired bodies and sore muscles after a

146

marathon night of love-making. Surrounded by the fragrant lush vegetation and the tranquil sounds of nature, we were again reminded of the beauty and healing power of the natural world. I encourage everyone to experience this molecule at some point in the setting of your favorite hot springs!

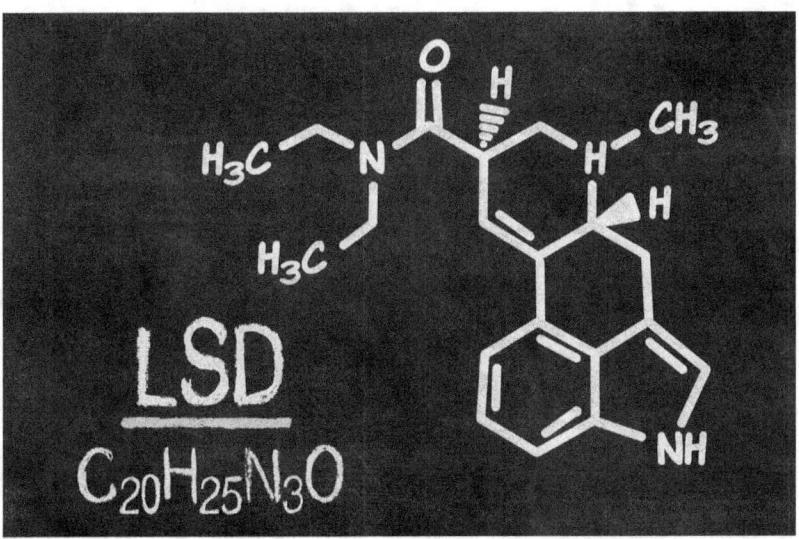

LSD Summary

How It Works

- Classic psychedelic ergoline contains rigidified phenethylamine and tryptamine backbones within chemical ring structure.

- Primary targets are 5HT1A/2A/2C receptors.

- Also interacts with dopamine (D1 and D2), adrenergic (α1A/2A), and 5HT2B receptors.

Metabolism of LSD

- Extensively metabolized by liver enzymes – 1% excreted unchanged.

- Several enzymes involved, CYP450, glucuronidases, peroxidases – not fully described.

- Primarily inactive metabolites although nor-LSD and hydroxyl-LSD have activity.

- 2-Oxo-3-hydroxy-LSD (O-H-LSD) major human metabolite of LSD.

Typical Dosing*

- Microdosing 5-25 μg

- Low 25-50 μg

- Moderate 50-200 μg

- High ≥ 300 μg

- Standard dose is 100-150 μg orally or sublingually

  *LSD is dosed in micrograms (ug) and 1000 ug is equal to a single milligram. This means that LSD is incredibly potent and cannot be accurately measured with normal jewelry scales (accurate to ~one mg). Serial dilution is necessary for accurate dosing. For these reasons LSD is often found in a liquid or on blotter paper.

Common Journey Experiences

- Empathogenic heart opening.

- Enhanced visualization of colors & sounds.

- Onset of effects ~30 to 60 minutes, peak effects ~two to four hours, total experience duration ~eight to 10 hours.

Potential Therapeutic Uses

LSD has not been employed in as many modern-day trials for treatment of illness relative to MDMA or psilocybin. This is perhaps due to its longer duration of action or lingering negative reputation from the 1960s. However, LSD is popular as a neurobiological probe into the mechanisms of psychedelics and is being developed for clinical use.

- Depression and Anxiety that is life-threatening.

- Alcohol Use Disorder.

- Cluster headaches.

Potential Adverse Effects

Physical

Nausea
Increased blood pressure & heart rate
Discomfort

Psych/Neuro

Transient anxiety
Emotional discomfort
Paranoia or confusion

Potential Drug Interactions & Contraindications

Drug Interactions

- Lithium → Increased risk of seizures or dysphoric experience quality, contraindicated.

- Chronic SSRI/SNRI or MAOI use → Possible diminished effects.

- Buspirone → Possible diminished effects.

- Acute MAOI use → Intensified psychedelic effects.

- Tricyclic Antidepressants → Intensified effects.

- Benzodiazepines → Possible diminished effects.

- Atypical antipsychotics → Reduced psychedelic effects.

- Triptan or ergoline migraine agents → Vasoconstriction and increased cardiovascular risks.

Contraindicated

- Bipolar I or severe bipolar conditions.
- Schizophrenia, psychosis, or psychotic conditions.

Legality

- LSD is regulated as illicit or Schedule I Substances by the United States federal government. However, the legal status of LSD can vary at the state level.

- LSD is illegal to manufacture, possess, distribute, or use under federal law.

- Some clinical trials and studies are ongoing to assess the safety and efficacy of LSD-assisted psychotherapy for conditions such as depression, anxiety, distress associated with life-threatening illness, alcohol use disorder, and cluster headaches.

References: 16, 17, 18, 19 & 20.

Chapter 8

Cannabis: An Ancient Healer to be Revered

I've had a nuanced relationship with Cannabis throughout my life. Most of it has been sporadic and minimalistic, as I didn't like the dampening cognitive effect on my brain. During my college days, I remember feeling this, and occasionally even had difficulty forming complete sentences after three to four hits. At the time, I felt its effects were somewhat akin to alcohol (*sans* motor incoordination that comes with booze) and preferred to experience insights, enlightenment, and visions from classic psychedelics, rather than turning my brain off to a degree with Cannabis or alcohol.

While many people like to consume Cannabis recreationally or as an alternative to alcohol, the psychedelic properties of Cannabis or THC make it a superior and safer option. As I maintained an open mind over the years, I began to re-introduce myself to the more esoteric blends and benefits of contemporary Cannabis products. I happily discovered the profound and sexually enhancing effects of Cannabis just five years ago. By paying close attention to dose, frequency of use, as well as set and setting, I've found that one can unlock altered states with Cannabis that are truly divine.

Cannabis can truly be psychedelic and I acknowledge the healing potentials of cannabidiol (CBD) and delta-9-tetrahydrocannabinol (THC) in the plant.[21] In fact, I've carried CBD tinctures, topical creams, and CBD gummies with melatonin in my office for several years and have documented benefits in the reduction of anxiety, pain, and improved sleep. This is so much better than having to prescribe pain medications or benzodiazepines that may tend to impair cognitive function while also reducing brain wave coherence between persons. They simply dumb and numb you down pharmacologically.

Before I dive into that more, here's some detail on Cannabis. Its psychedelic effects are primarily derived from its psychoactive compound, THC. However, other cannabinoids and terpenes also play an important role, especially in balancing or shaping the effects of THC. This is commonly known as the "entourage effect."[22] The ratios of CBD to THC, for example, can play a major role in stimulating optimal libido and sensual flow with your lover.

Cultural Origins

Cannabis is believed to have originated in Central Asia, specifically in the region that is now modern-day Mongolia and southern Siberia. It is thought to have been used for its medicinal and psychoactive properties by ancient cultures in this area as early as 500 BC. From there, the use of Cannabis spread to other parts of Asia, the Middle East, and eventually to Europe and the Americas.

Cannabis in the United States

Cannabis became more mainstream in the United States during the counterculture movement of the 1960s and 1970s. It was embraced by the hippie movement and became associated with rebellion, creativity, and alternative lifestyles. Fast forward to 2025---marijuana is now legal in 38 states and the District of Columbia (DC), recreational use of marijuana is legal in 24 stated and in DC. Over this period, Cannabis plants have been selectively bred for particular properties, cannabinoid, or terpene profiles. This has resulted in myriad "strains" of Cannabis that are generally much stronger or higher in THC content relative to Cannabis of the past. Higher potency Cannabis and the expansion of concentrated products (wax, shatter, hash, etc.) provide the potential for powerful non-ordinary states in which "set and setting" becomes a critical factor in experience quality. For example, the use of high-potency Cannabis in uncontrolled environments often leads to panic or "ego-death" type experiences that are not dissimilar to reports of psilocybin use in similar environments.

What altered states can one expect with Cannabis?

- Euphoria: Feeling happy and relaxed.

- Altered perceptions of time: Time may accelerate or slow down, similar to other psychedelics.

- Enhanced sensations: This can be particularly profound in terms of increased sexual sensitivity, as well as enhancement to skin touch, colors, and taste. Your mango may taste twice as good, and you'll also want to eat twice as much of it!

- Altered sense of self: Some of you may feel more introspective and meditative, while others may feel more social and extroverted.

- Visual and auditory hallucinations/visions: Light visuals may appear similar to psychedelics, but tend to be more organic for me. For example, patterns of leaves, ferns, floral colors, and softer more organic geometry, compared to the more angular geometry such as hexagons seen with LSD. Some may appreciate enhancements in the music they are listening to and rarely have auditory hallucinations. All of this occurs at higher doses of THC.

- Anxiety and paranoia: Some individuals may experience this and will need to keep doses low, avoid this plant altogether, or consider exploring in guided settings, to help calm anxiety.

What are the primary components of Cannabis and the characteristic sensations and benefits they offer?

- **Indica strains of Cannabis** are often associated with relaxation, sedation, and a bodily high. These effects may offer a more meditative and introspective experience and are my favorite for psychedelic sacred sexual flow. They typically carry a more "skunk" like smell and are rich in terpenes such as beta myrcene or linalool.

- **Sativa strains of Cannabis** in contrast are associated with more energy, creativity, and a head high. Elevation of mood is more common and these strains typically carry a more citrus or pine-like smell and are rich in terpenes such as limonene or alpha-pinene.

- **CBD** (cannabidiol) is the non-psychedelic component that doesn't produce a noticeable "high" when consumed, although it is psychoactive, given its efficacy as an antiepileptic. Over the past several years, it has gained significant attention due to its potential therapeutic anti-inflammatory, neurological, and anxiolytic benefits. Some studies suggest that CBD may help with conditions like anxiety, chronic pain, and epilepsy, but research is ongoing. On average, most traditional strains of Cannabis used for recreational purposes contain higher levels of THC and might have anywhere from 0.1% to 3% CBD. However, strains bred for medicinal purposes can have CBD content as high as 10% to 20%, or even higher in some specialized strains.

- **CBN**—This cannabinoid is unique because it is not produced directly by the Cannabis plant. Instead, it is the degradation product of THC (tetrahydrocannabinol, the psychoactive component in marijuana). CBN forms when THC is exposed to heat and light over time. As marijuana ages, some of the THC breaks down into CBN.

Our explorations to experience the psychedelic effects of Cannabis began by trying vape pens of the indica and sativa varieties. We noticed light effects with each and a bit more with the combo. We then experimented with five to 10 mg of edible indica gummies to see if this might offer more and were pleasantly surprised! Light to moderate psychedelic geometry popped with the indicia alone!

To gain more insights and depth of knowledge around psychedelic journeys with Cannabis, I sat down with Daniel McQueen,
director of The Center for Medicinal Mindfulness, based in
Boulder, Colorado. It is one of the first legal psychedelic therapy
clinics in North America. An expert on psychedelic journeys,
Daniel recommends considering an "Alchemy blend" of Sativa,
Indica, and CBN for optimal psychedelic effects. Daniel prefers
using flowers, since dosing can be controlled more readily than
edibles in a circle or alone. More detail on his recommended optimal dosing and blends can be found in his comprehensive book,
*Psychedelic Cannabis, Therapeutic Methods and Unique Blends to
Treat Trauma and Transform Consciousness.*[23] In general, he feels
that lightweights like myself can drop in well with 10 to 20 mg
(a few tokes) of Cannabis, while others may need 30 to 40 mg,
and those who are more regular users could need as much as 80
to 100 mg.

After talking to Daniel and reading his book, we tried an edible
gummy combo, taking five mg of each of the three: Indica/Sativa/
CBN per his "Alchemy Blend," and experienced a trifecta of
moderate psychedelic effects, huge libido boost, and sexual sensitivity increase. We found that the more rapid-release gummies
that take effect in 15 to 30 minutes are the easiest to work with
and provide a good three to four hour duration of fun. Libido
and sexual sensitivity peaks at about an hour, creating an opportunity for multiple orgasms. Since we are occasional connoisseurs
of Cannabis, the dose needed for us is in the low range of 15 to
20 mg. Others may need 40 mg or more, but start low and work
yourself up slowly and safely. Keep a journal on dosing and the
experience for future reference.

Bella and I have been performing ongoing fieldwork and have found the rapid-release edibles to be the best for psychedelic sacred flow, since we don't have to stop and vape or smoke flower, given the longer duration of action of gummies.

The onset begins in 30 minutes to two hours, depending on the edible release form, but again, the benefits of duration and intensity of the journey are superior by not having to stop frequently for more inhaled THC. Another reason edibles are better is due to the conversion of THC in the liver to 11-hydroxy-thc, which has greater psychedelic effects. Some may find inhaling is their preferred route regardless, so personal preference is best. Find what works best for you. Inhaled can be used as an occasional short-term booster after the full effects of an oral dose are not achieved.

Remember to always start at low doses and work your way up only after an edible has peaked. Too much THC can throw you off, and finding the right dose, strain, or blends can take some personal R&D. Recent research in 2023 has shown that daily Cannabis can increase our risk for stroke and heart attacks.

"After adjusting for age, sex, and major cardiovascular risk factors, the results indicated that daily Cannabis users were 34% more likely to have Coronary Artery Disease (CAD) than those who have never used marijuana," according to the American College of Cardiology in a February 2023 press release titled, "Frequent Marijuana Use Linked to Heart Disease." It cited studies and said, "In contrast, *monthly* Cannabis use *was not associated* with a significant increase in the risk of CAD."[24]

Most researchers believe that oral is safer, since it doesn't have the harmful chemical byproducts of combustion that may be found in flower or vape pens, but more research is needed to confirm this opinion. Frequent THC use may cause inflammation to the lining of our vessels, whether oral or inhaled.

The take-home message at this point is: Use THC in moderation like anything else. Consider daily Coq10 for vascular health if you are a regular user of THC. Rotate journeys with THC with other psychedelics to cross-train your brain and to avoid a loss of responsiveness. Keep a journal and record your doses and high-light the dose that gives you optimal flow.

More Cannabis tips:

- Create the set and setting you desire prior to the drop-in to facilitate intimate flow.

- Set intentions for yourself, and as a couple.

- Start low and go slow. If you're new to Cannabis, begin with a dose that provides 2.5 to 5 mg of THC. Be patient with the process and realize that it may take a few journeys to find optimal dosing for both of you. For us, 10 to 15 mg edible dose is best.

- Flower or vape pens may be used instead, or as a booster as needed after a couple hours of allowing the oral to take full effect.

- Wait a couple of hours before adding more edibles, unless you are using a rapid release, in which one hour may be adequate to do another dose.

- Increase incrementally by just 2.5 to 5 mg.

- Again, remember to journal the doses, strains, brand used, and how you responded for future reference.

- Integrate your experience together the following day and as often as needed.

- For purposes relating to sacred sexuality, focus on "ritual" as opposed to "habitual" use.

- Habitual use may down-regulate your response, so if possible, use more intermittently to promote a more profound mind-expanding psychedelic experience.

Cannabis Craziness!

Bella has become a huge fan of our Cannabis journeys lately, especially since she loves the enhanced sexual sensitivity.

One Friday eve, we decided to do a combination of 5 mg Indica/10 mg Sativa and 5 mg CBN by edible rapid release. We dialed in a tantric playlist on Spotify, lit a few candles, dimmed the lights, brought the hot stone massage warmer to the bedside, and quickly got naked. Within 20 minutes, we both began to feel our heart rates increase, along with a desire to ravage each other. Bella was especially frisky and I could feel her wanting to be somewhat of a dominatrix this eve! She positioned herself on top of me and began to passionately kiss me, then dangled her breasts over my lips, teasing me more. Placing my lips around them, I gave her nipples some gentle love bites, then circled my tongue around them broadly. Watching her nipples firm up and seeing them glisten in the flickering candlelight was super-arousing. Soon she hopped off me and I heard her rustling around the bed.

"What are ya up to, Bella?"

"I'm digging around for the restraints tied to the corners of your bed! Found 'em!"

Hmm, this is gonna be a wild ride! I thought.

Within a few minutes, she had me tied up tight in four-point restraints with me looking up at the ceiling. Placing an eye mask over me, she then plotted a strategy to drive me, and her, off the edge.

"I want you to receive a tantric massage while I've restrained you and I'll take my creativity from there, baby," said Bella.

"Mmm, so loving this already baby!" I said.

She started by pouring some warm massage oil on my navel, then flowed her hands gently up to my chest and neck, massaging me in her intuitive way. Her hand began to amplify and connect my chakras more deeply. Periodically, she'd surprise me with the tip of her tongue touching my lips as she continued to slowly flow her love and energy into me with her hands.

"This is so amazing, Bella, sometimes I feel guilty about receiving so much from you, but when 'ya have me tied up, I have no choice!"

"Don't worry Astraeus, this is your turn to receive, and if you'd like you can return the love to me later with or without restraints."

Completely letting go and trusting her flow gave me a more profound heart-based connection to her. The element of trusted vulnerability, combined with an excitement of not knowing what was coming next, created a nice dopamine rush. On top of all this, the Cannabis was kicking in more and I was beginning to appreciate greater skin sensitivity, heightening libido, and subtle geometry emerging visually, as she continued to torture me with her love.

Soon I heard her hands reaching into the water to retrieve the polished labradorite hot stones. She placed them along my chakras, including one under me at the base of my spine for my root chakra. Labradorite is known for its energetic properties that enhance all chakras.

According to Robert Simmons, "Labradorite is an interdimensional stone, emanating an energy which helps one to consciously pierce the veil between our waking world and the many domains and planes of inner awareness."[25]

Embracing the luminous energies emanating from the gemstones, I surrendered to their healing flow. Bella's hands, aglow with a radiant light, danced gracefully over me, channeling an ethereal warmth. The plant medicine, infused with the essence of the Gaia, coursed through me, opening my chakras even further. As these elements converged, I found myself transcending the physical realm, entering an otherworldly dimension where time and space blurred, and my consciousness expanded into new realms of perception and understanding. In this interdimensional space, a profound sense of peace and enlightenment enveloped me, revealing the interconnected tapestry of life and energy.

Floating in this space, I began to feel Bella flow her hands with more massage oil between my legs, and around my root chakra. My Kundalini energy began to amplify with this, making me squirm and pull on the restraints around my ankles and wrists.

Working her hands gracefully and slowly around my perineum and my genitals, she sent me into an ecstatic state of pleasure. Soon she was teasing the tip of my penis with her tongue, then took all of me in her mouth as she tortured me to the edge of orgasm, then backing off. Seeking some pleasure for herself, she surprised me as she positioned her yoni over my face.

I could feel her wet yoni and clitoris on my lips, dying for attention.

Running my tongue wildly around her clitoris, she lightly pushed towards me harder. Unable to use my restrained hands, she strategically moved her perineum to flow with my dancing tongue. I could feel and taste her yummy juiciness as she was climbing closer to a climax. Within minutes, she released with a screaming orgasm as I felt her squirting on my face. Feeling her legs tremor next to my shoulders, she held her yoni within tongue's length.

"Bella, place your clit on my third eye," I said.

"Mmm, here 'ya go! Whoa, so much energy flowing into me from your third eye, baby!" said Bella.

"OMFG, I am feeling pulses of energy flowing from your root chakra into me as well. It's wild to feel a link from your fiery root chakra into my upper chakras. Hold this for a while."

"Astraeus, I just want to let you know that that was one of the most astral, off-planet orgasms I've ever had."

"Bella, I so felt that when you released on my face!"

After a few minutes, she changed position, and I felt her directing my throbbing cock into her yoni. Riding me slowly, then a little faster, she brought me to the verge of releasing again.

"How does this feel, babe?" Bella asked.

"As much as I want to orgasm, being on the verge like this is pure ecstasy!"

"Don't worry," she said, "just another five to 10 minutes, and I'll make you explode."

I could feel her turn around to face towards my feet, followed by placing me inside her again. Starting slowly again, she quickly accelerated as I felt her ass bouncing down on me. Soon, we were both moaning in ecstasy and orgasmed wildly together. Sitting with me inside her, I could feel her still coming as she contracted around me.

"Wow, wow, wow! Can we make this happen every night?" I asked.

"Sure, but next time I wanna roll you over and spank 'ya good with the whip!" said Bella. She removed the velcro constraints from my extremities, the mask off my face, and looked into my eyes passionately while wildly saying, "That was beyond fun!!"

Summary

Cannabis is a powerful ancient plant medicine that offers so much more than what many consider a classic high (e.g. "couch-locked" with the munchies). Holding it in a sacred, heart-centered space with intentions to find enlightenment with your lover can be expansive and healing. We've found that it takes a fair amount of experimentation to find the perfect dosing and the strains that work best. The more rapid-release edibles work best and have the most profound effects on our libido and desires to be in states of passionate love together. A balanced ratio of THC to CBD may promote better sexual flow by keeping you more relaxed and in flow. Too much THC can occasionally impair your sexual flow if it creates anxiety or paranoia. Some companies produce edibles that include aphrodisiac herbs that can further catalyze the THC and CBD, or you can take them separately. Blue Lotus tincture and others are worth experimenting with.

One more insight to share. As I alluded to earlier, I theorize that stimulating our brains with various psychedelics over time may epigenetically shift our neural tracts for improved sensitivity to other plant medicines.

For advanced psychonauts, Cannabis can be added in low doses to amplify other plant medicines or synthetic molecule journeys as it tends to "play well" with others. I've found that adding 2-5mg of cannabis gummies to a 2-CB journey can be profound. Visuals and sexual sensitivity are both enhanced. Typically a combo of rapid release Sativa/Indica at 2.5mg each is perfect. The following chart summarizes some of the neurotransmitter impacts.

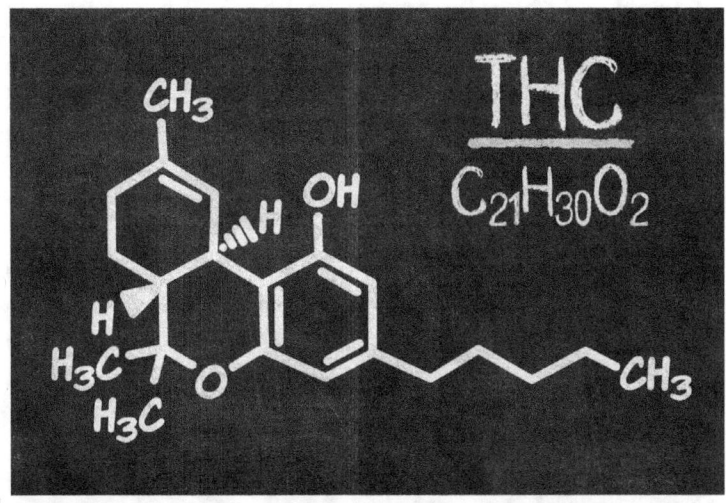

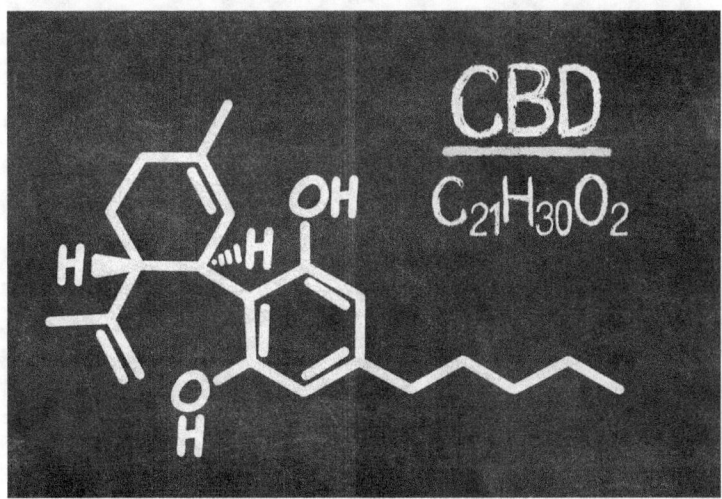

Cannabis and THC Summary

How It Works

- THC is a partial agonist of cannabinoid 1 and 2 (CB1 and CB2) receptors, although activity at CB1 receptors is more important to psychoactive effects.

Metabolism of THC

- CYP2C9 and CYP3A4 are the primary enzymes involved in metabolizing THC, although CYP2C19 may also play a role.

Typical Dosing*

- Low 2.5-5 mg
- Moderate 5-20 mg
- **High ≥ 20 mg**
- The standard oral dose is 5 to 10 mg of THC

  *Persons who use Cannabis regularly often have tolerance to its effects and some persons may be able to tolerate doses much higher than others.

Common Journey Experiences

- Increased tactile sensation, a feeling of time passing differently.
- Enhanced visualization of colors & sounds.
- Onset of effects for oral THC ~30 to 60 min, peak effects ~two to four hours, total experience duration ~eight hours.
- Onset of effects for inhaled THC <15 seconds, peak effects five to 15 min, total experience duration one to two hours.

Potential Therapeutic Uses

Cannabinoids and THC have varying degrees of evidence and are popularly used for a number of indications. Some of the better researched uses are:

- Appetite regulation and prevention of cachectic wasting.

- Reduction of nausea or emesis association with chemotherapy.

- Reduction of muscle spasticity in neurodegenerative illness (e.g. Multiple Sclerosis),

- Chronic pain.

  Reference: 26

Potential Adverse Effects

Physical

Increased blood pressure & heart rate
Conjunctivitis (red eyes)
Xerostomia (dry mouth)
Increased appetite

Psych/Neuro

Transient anxiety
Emotional discomfort
Paranoia or confusion

Potential Drug Interactions & Contraindications

Cannabis and cannabinoids likely carry clinically significant drug interaction potential under certain circumstances and not others, For example, dose, route of administration, and frequency of use are all likely major factors in whether there's a drug interaction that is "significant" or not.

Drug Interactions

- THC concentrations can be increased by strong CYP3A4 inhibitors (verapamil, clarithromycin) and decreased by strong CYP3A4 inductors (rifampicin, carbamazepine).

- THC and CBD inhibit CYP2C9 and CYP3A4 although they may not produce clinically relevant drug interactions with doses of THC < 30 mg/day or CBD doses < 300 mg/day.

- Smoking Cannabis can induce CYP1A2 metabolism which could diminish concentrations of drugs such as theophylline, clozapine, or olanzapine.

- Other additive effects (cardiovascular, psychoactive) are possible with use of other drugs that raise cardiovascular parameters or have pronounced psychoactivity.

References: 27, 28.

Contraindicated

- Bipolar I or severe bipolar conditions.
- Schizophrenia, psychosis, or psychotic conditions.
- Cannabinoid hyperemesis syndrome.

Legality

While THC and Cannabis remain illegal at the federal level and the DOJ/DEA did interfere with state programs at one time, the Rohrabacher–Farr Amendment was passed by Congress in 2014 to bar the DOJ from spending funds on prosecutions and asset forfeiture actions against medical marijuana patients and providers, including businesses that operate legally under state law.

- Medical Marijuana: Some states have legalized medical marijuana, which allows patients with qualifying medical conditions to use products that contain THC for therapeutic purposes.

- Recreational Marijuana: Some states have legalized recreational marijuana, which allows anyone over the age of 21 to purchase marijuana with no medical indication.

- Several states have decriminalized the possession of small amounts of marijuana, reducing the penalties associated with personal use.

Chapter 9

Ketamine:

A Molecule for Inward Growth, Balance, and Interdimensional Travel with Your Lover

Ketamine is a molecule that can be used for profound inward work, thus making you a better lover, especially if it helps you address any anxiety, depression, PTSD, or even OCD. It can give individuals a much deeper understanding of themselves as they typically flow into a blissful happy space. The experience can bring in visuals of magnificent landscapes, matrix-like visuals, psychedelic geometry, portals, expansive heart opening, and more. Like plant medicines and other molecules, every journey is unique. Finding the optimal dose with your practitioner takes time. The initial calculation of the dose is based on your weight, but is often adjusted up or down based on your response, especially if you are still too "in your head" during the journey. Oftentimes, one feels a clearing of negative energies and a weight being lifted off their shoulders.

On rare occasions, one can have a dark vision, but this can usually be cleared by breath, sound healing, or energy work by a competent facilitator. Using this molecule in a medical setting is recommended with a facilitator or therapist trained in Ketamine-assisted psychotherapy. They can screen you for contraindications and monitor your blood pressure, which can become elevated during a session.

Many folks are buying Ketamine on the streets unfortunately. Be safe. It is not worth risking the potential risks of it being laced with fentanyl, etc. It also has significant addiction potential.

The journey with Ketamine is typically about an hour long and is dosed based on your weight initially, then adjusted in future sessions to achieve optimal outcomes. Ketamine is bioavailable by many routes of administration and is administered in a number of ways. For example, many Ketamine centers are administering intramuscular (IM) injections as the main route, but offer intravenous (IV) for severe depression and suicidality, as it offers better efficacy relative to intranasal esketamine (Spravato)[29].

Sublingual lozenges or troches may be offered too, and in patients who are well screened and appropriate, it may be used at home with regular follow-up. Home Ketamine therapy should never be prescribed to individuals with a history of drug abuse, especially to those with a history of opioid addiction. They should be recommended to use psilocybin as an alternative.

Couples therapy is available at some centers and can allow therapists to ask more questions during the lighter stages of the journey helping them clear deep-seated emotions, unresolved issues, and patterns of behavior that may make a relationship difficult. A lower dose for the whole session can also be used for Ketamine Assisted Psychotherapy (KAP).

Ketamine was discovered in 1962 by a scientist named Calvin Stevens at the Parke-Davis Laboratories, which is now a part of Pfizer. In 1965, it was approved by the U.S. Food and Drug Administration (FDA) for human use. It was initially used as a general anesthetic in medical and veterinary settings. Its unique properties, such as providing both anesthesia and analgesia (pain relief), made it particularly useful for surgical procedures. It has also been used as an anesthetic for children and in emergency medicine, due to its rapid onset of action.

However, Ketamine's use expanded beyond anesthesia. In the 1970s, it gained popularity as a recreational drug due to its dissociative and hallucinogenic effects. It was used recreationally under various street names like "Special K" or "Ket."

In the early 2000s, rapid and robust antidepressant effects were noted in preliminary trials conducted at the National Institute of Mental Health (NIMH) using a 0.5mg/kg IV infusion over 40 minutes. However, it was the FDA's approval of esKetamine (a nasal spray and the S-enantiomer of racemic Ketamine) that marked a significant milestone. esKetamine, under the brand name Spravato, was approved by the FDA in March 2019 for treatment-resistant depression in conjunction with an oral antidepressant. It's important to note that the approval of esKetamine is distinct from Ketamine itself, though they are related compounds.

The use of regular Ketamine for depression in "Ketamine clinics" is considered off-label, as racemic Ketamine itself has not received FDA approval specifically for depression treatment.

Even though regular (racemic) Ketamine has not received approval from the FDA for depression, it is more effective and is the most common, more economical form utilized in the outpatient clinical setting.

Today, it continues to be used as an anesthetic in both human and veterinary medicine and is also being studied for its potential therapeutic effects in treating conditions like Post-Traumatic Stress Disorder (PTSD) and chronic pain. Early studies have also shown that Ketamine might provide rapid, albeit temporary, relief from OCD symptoms. However, these findings are based on relatively small-scale studies, and more extensive research is needed to determine the long-term benefits, appropriate dosing, and potential side effects. More research is needed, but because regular Ketamine is generically available, it will be difficult to find funding beyond the NIH or private altruistic funding.

How does Ketamine work?

Theoretically, it's thought to work through the modulation of the glutamate system, which is a key neurotransmitter involved in learning and memory. By blocking the NMDA receptor (N-methyl-D-aspartate), it leads to the release of glutamate. This receptor enhances synaptic (neural connections) plasticity, which then promotes new neural connections. This activity, combined with its ability to increase BDNF (Brain-derived neurotrophic factor), makes it a rock star for neuroplasticity (reorganizing, and promoting new neural pathways) and thus may help us with more creativity and better cognitive function. Research is being conducted looking at Ketamine benefits in the treatment of Alzheimer's and Parkinson's. They hypothesize that the benefits of neuroplasticity, BDNF stimulation, NMDA receptor modulation, and anti-inflammatory effects may slow or reverse cognitive decline. (cit 1,2)

Weaving Ketamine into our lives for greater intimacy, and psychological well-being.

Bella and I have been working with sublingual Ketamine lozenges for a few years now in a mindful, safe way for mood enhancement and enlightenment. We both obtain it legally from a therapist and prescribing psychiatrist who believes in its benefits way beyond its use for depression, seeing its expanded potential to promote optimal mental health. In this way, it could be seen as a proactive, preventative approach to promoting mental well-being. In addition to facilitating mindfulness and healthy relationships, and reducing anxiety and depression, we can also use psychedelics to help us stay even-keeled, open-minded, and loving. All while simultaneously promoting neuroplasticity, positive epigenetic shifts, and new neural connections.

Our personal application in addition to this, applies to the realm of couples therapy aimed at deepening intimacy and travels into oneness together. We often alternate our intentions between doing inward work side by side or setting an intention to flow into oneness and love together. On rare occasions, we can do both. We limit the use to a few times a month to avoid any risks of addiction or less responsiveness to this molecule.

A night to send love and healing to our troubled world.

"Love is the bridge between you and everything."

—Rumi

In the fall of 2023, Bella and I were struggling emotionally while witnessing the ongoing conflicts between Israel and Hamas. Seeing and hearing the thousands of innocent civilians being slaughtered on both sides via newsfeeds was creating stress, sadness, and deep feelings of empathy. Coupled with the frustration of not being able to visualize a short- or long-term peaceful resolution and the fear of what's next, we decided to make a deep dive together to explore these emotions.

Together, we set an intention to help us both let go of the accumulated stress from the war, and then if possible towards the end of the journey come together to collectively send light to the region to promote peace and healing.

We selected a playlist together from Spotify curated for sublingual Ketamine, that included some Native American flute music, blended with world music. Lighting a Palo Santo-scented candle across the room, we laid down in bed with our eyes closed in the dimly lit room.

Placing a 150mg compounded Ketamine troche between our cheek and gums, we began to taste the bitter flavor of K releasing, somewhat attenuated by the mint flavor added by the pharmacy. Within 30 minutes or so, we began to feel the familiar dampening of both our stress and busy minds. At an hour, I began to see matrix-like geometry that would periodically morph into lightly colored shifting kaleidoscope-like images. As I was deeply dropped in, I opened my eyes momentarily and noticed that the ceiling was gone and the stars were visible above.

I flowed into an expansive state of heart opening and love, feeling connected to all that is. Staying in the timeless realm, I eventually had some awareness of our original intention coming into me. We both spontaneously spoke saying, "We are one." Then, we chanted "oneness" for a few minutes, feeling ourselves connecting to all that is in the field of love. This amplified the spectrum and vibrancy of a tapestry-like pattern of colors we were both seeing with our eyes closed. Feeling Bella in a coherent space with me, I spoke softly to her, saying, "Let's send unconditional love and healing to the Middle East to promote peace and the end of this conflict."

She replied with a simple, "Yes."

We sat up, a bit wobbly in the bed, and I had her sit on my crossed legs, facing me in the Yab-Yum position. Feeling our hearts connect, I visualized them connecting, then spiraling and flowing our divine masculine and feminine energies up and around our planet. As we surrounded it with this field, I visualized it flowing back down to the Middle East, Ukraine, and other regions in need of healing light.

Holding my heart closer to hers and our foreheads together, I asked, "What are you feeling, Bella?"

"I'm just feeling my heart so wide open and a healing energy flowing between us and emanating healing light around the world."

"Perfect, let's just hold that space for our planet as long as we can."

Holding this meditative state for quite some time, I felt a deepening of our bond as we extended ourselves together way beyond the personal level, to a higher dimensional frequency of universal love. This particular experience soared us to such a high level of ecstatic oneness together, that in many ways it exceeded an orgasmic experience. Who knew this could be possible?

Integrating our journey over breakfast the following day with her, I began to realize the deeper, more profound benefit of being in a sacred sexual relationship with her. Having learned to go deep and interdimensional with her over the years, we have developed a powerful partnership to collectively send light to others. The power of a couple regardless of sexual orientation can flow the energies of divine masculine and feminine in ways more profound than in solo meditation. If we can amplify the frequency of love, from meditative states of sacred union, in sacred circles, or a collective consciousness as an individual with others, I truly feel we can change the world.

The challenge lies in going to that space of unconditional, ego-free love. I feel that it is best achieved with psychedelics in a sacred set and setting, breathwork, or by a devotional life in a monastery, ashram, or other deeply spiritual meditative center. The first option is easiest. Religious communities, unfortunately, have their own ego-identity, biases, and agendas, thus making pure unconditional love difficult for those who don't align with their prophets, Gods, or messiahs. Thus, finding an unbiased coherent field of love, healing, and unity in our world of diverse cultures and religions seems difficult for most.

Either we naturally awaken to this state of unconditional love, or we realize that suddenly Earth may go through a mass extinction event if we don't see the light and come together. Examples of how we might be forced to come together include uniting our world-wide resources to take down a large asteroid capable of eliminating all planetary life, or a threatening alien visitor from another galaxy who has witnessed enough human exploitation of the planet and arrives to solve that problem overnight. Of course the obvious threats of climate change, nuclear war, more lethal pandemics, and resource depletion present enough threats to our existence without a giant asteroid hitting Kansas City. I firmly believe that intelligent life exists from other planets, galaxies, or dimensions, but I also intuitively feel most are here to protect us. Maybe there are opportunities for us to foster collaborative relationships with more intelligent beings and solve our global threats. Perhaps it's already happening and our government hasn't disclosed it. If not, maybe we can create an altruistic form of artificial intelligence that can sustain, rather than destroy us.

Imagine what would happen if intelligent life from another galaxy arrived and informed us that they are our creators. How would the priests and leaders of world religions react if the visitors provided clear proof to demonstrate this? Luckily we have bold individuals like Steven Greer, MD, a retired physician who founded the Center for the Study of Extraterrestrial Intelligence (CSETI) and the Disclosure Project, and David Grusch, former Air Force Intelligence officer, Representative of the National Reconnaissance Office to the Unidentified Aerial Phenomena (UAP) Task Force, who are working to release classified documents on UAP's and more to the public soon. Unfortunately, many still laugh at the idea of intelligent life beyond our planet, likely since the government wants the general public to remain dumbed down and ignorant. It's time for all of us to realize that we are not alone.

In summary, Ketamine, like other psychedelics, can help us let go of preferential cultural bias and expand it to be all-inclusive to everyone on the planet, and even expand it to hypothetical beings beyond our galaxy. Creating this unbiased field of love may have the potential to shift dark fields of incoherent light to a coherent light of healing. Perhaps our light may impact others' perspectives in a positive manner, improving happiness and sustainability for all on this planet. While collective consciousness has not been scientifically linked to "quantum entanglement theory," I feel there is a high potential for it to be demonstrated as technology and artificial intelligence advances. While this may sound like metaphysical bullshit, if we can't find a way to evolve into this higher vibrational state, we will become extinct from the myriad of existing threats to our planet.

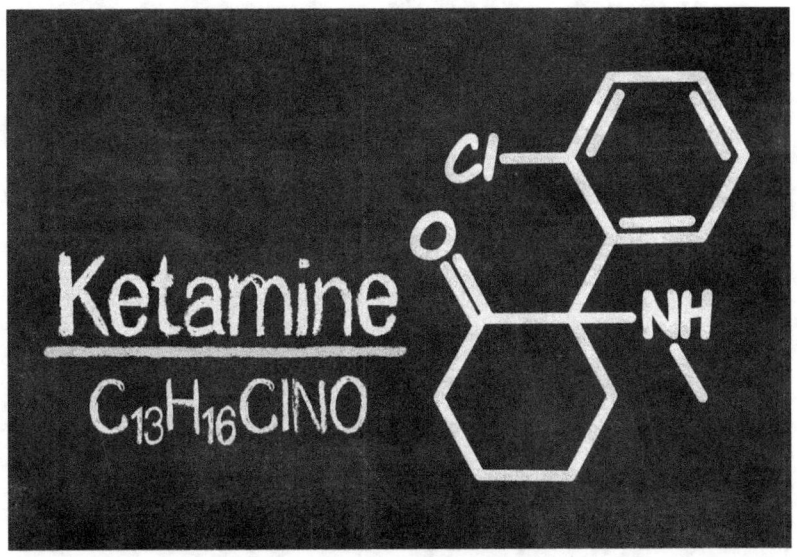

Ketamine Summary

How It Works

- Arylcyclohexylamine dissociative anesthetic.

- Non-competitive glutamate antagonist at NMDA receptors.

- Available as racemic formulation of R-Ketamine and S-Ketamine or intranasal formulation of S-Ketamine.

- Racemic and S-Ketamine formulations may differ in therapeutic or adverse effects.

Duration of Journey

- Hepatically metabolized by CYP3A4/5, CYP2B6, and CYP2C9.

- First-pass metabolism and kinetics may depend on the route of administration.

- Journey/session duration of 2 to 4 hours. Varies with mode administered. For example, with IM (intramuscular injection) most of the deep journey is finished within an hour, and then you are in a blissful relaxed state as the Ketamine is cleared over the next few hours.

Typical Dosing

Variable, depending on use purpose and route of administration. Usually used 2-3x/week for two to four weeks during induction of treatment for Treatment-Resistant Depression (TRD).

- 0.5 mg/kg IV infusion over 40 minutes.

- 56 or 84 mg intranasal (IN) esKetamine

- 0.25-1 mg/kg IM or SC injection

Common Journey Experiences

- Provides an opportunity to let go of stress, negativity, traumas, and the weight of the world around us.

- Going to a place of blissful love.

- Geometrical imagery, images of nature, matrix-like imagery, filmstrip-like imagery, and portals are possible at higher doses.

- At higher doses, flowing into oneness, dissolving your ego.

- Improved mood and reduced anxiety.

- Caution—Please do not take this or any other sedating psychedelic or medication in a bathtub, pool, or hottub. We saw what happened to the "Friends" actor when he did.

Potential Therapeutic Uses

- Treatment Resistant Depression (TRD) in persons with unipolar or bipolar depression.

- Depressive symptoms in persons with suicidal ideation.

- Off-label or experimentally used for PTSD, anxiety disorders, pain conditions, and substance use disorder (cocaine).

Potential Adverse Effects

Physical

Nausea
Increased blood pressure and heart rate
Lower Urinary Tract Symptoms*

Psych/Neuro

Dizziness, vertigo
Ataxia or motor incoordination
Dysgeusia (weird tastes)
Cognitive changes and dissociation
Sedation/headache
Habit-forming/addiction*

* Not common in therapeutic settings, frequent use of higher doses or Ketamine use disorder are most associated with development of LUTS, although it is possible and has been reported even with therapeutic dosing regimens.

Potential Drug Interactions & Contraindications

- Benzodiazepines, Lamotrigine, Clozapine → Diminishes effect of Ketamine.

- Opioids, Benzodiazepines, Alcohol, or GHB → Increased sedation effects, increased ataxia, dizziness, nausea, or emesis.

- CYP3A4/5, CYP2B6, and CYP2C9 Inhibitors → Increased blood concentrations.

- CYP3A4/5, CYP2B6, and CYP2C9 Inducers → Decreased blood concentrations.

Legality

- Legal in the United States and most countries under physician supervision/prescribing as a Schedule III medication.

- Illegal in the US and most countries for recreational production and use.

Chapter 10

Ayahuasca: A Profound Plant Medicine Healer from the Amazon

I've been blessed to have the honor of being in both Ayahuasca and Peyote ceremonial circles for almost 20 years. The healings and insights I've encountered with them have been profound.

This book partly owes its existence to the profound wisdom imparted by these plant teachers and the shamans who shared with me their knowledge and higher dimensional energies in sacred circles. There is a field of illumination created by them and the collective energy of those in the circle is something that one has to experience. If called, and you haven't experienced these particular circles, I hope you will someday manifest this journey. For this reason, I feel these plant medicines should be held in a set and setting administered in a sacred circle with the deepest respect by the Indigenous curandero (male) or curandera (female) for Ayahuasca.

I've found that Ayahuasca offers opportunities for profound inward work, while at the same time connecting us deeper to Mother Gaia and the cosmos. This plant teacher and many other psychedelic plant medicines and molecules can then further accelerate our spiritual growth while optimizing our energy balance and light body to be better lovers and stewards of the world.

Ayahuasca

Ayahuasca is a traditional psychoactive brew with roots from the Indigenous peoples of the Amazon Basin in South America—particularly Peru, Brazil, Colombia, and Ecuador. The name is derived from Quechua words "aya" meaning spirit or ancestor, and "huasca" meaning vine. So it is considered the "vine of the spirits."

Ayahuasca.

The brew has been used in shamanic circles for centuries in the Amazon Basin for healing, personal growth, and inward work. In the 1950s, it was discussed by William Burroughs and Allen Ginsberg as they shared their experiences in writings to the public.

Ayahuasca has gained major popularity in the last decade with psychedelic tourism, particularly to retreat centers outside of Iquitos, but also outside of Cusco in the Sacred Valley region.

Religious groups, such as Santo Daime and Uniao do Vegetal, have incorporated this plant medicine into their rituals for spiritual enlightenment within the practice of Christianity.

Pharmacological Action:

Ayahuasca is made by brewing both the Banisteriopsis caapi vine and the leaves of the Chacruna (Psychotria viridis plant), though other plants can sometimes be included. Here is a quick breakdown of the pharmacologic magic in these plants:

- **Chacruna** (Psychotria viridis) contains N,N-Dimethyl-tryptamine (DMT), a powerful psychoactive substance. DMT is a tryptamine alkaloid, similar in structure to serotonin, and it affects the brain by binding to serotonin receptors. On its own, if ingested orally, DMT is deactivated by the enzyme monoamine oxidase (found in our stomach), rendering it non-psychoactive.

- **Banisteriopsis caapi vine** contains beta-carbolines like harmine, harmaline, and tetrahydroharmine, which act as monoamine oxidase inhibitors (MAOIs). These MAOIs temporarily reduce the stomach's ability to break down DMT, allowing it to enter the bloodstream and eventually the brain, where it can exert its psychoactive effects for four to six hours.

- **Plant Synergy**: The shamanic blend of the DMT vine with the MAOI leaves of Chacruna in the brew gifts ceremony participants a prolonged, intense, and often profoundly introspective or visionary experience. Most will feel the effects within an hour and continue to feel them for four to six hours after consuming a reasonable amount. How shamans figured out the benefits of combining these plants together, picking them from over 80,000 known species in the rainforest, has been the subject of much debate. Participants may see beautiful geometry, gain insights into personal issues, experience deep emotional release, and on some occasions, see plants, jaguars, snakes, or other animals. Fields of energy are often noted around fellow participants and the surrounding forest. I've often seen these fields looking like a webbed geometric dome covering them. It is somewhat like a geodesic dome, but it flows more organically over the shaman or a group of them.

- **Plant Essence/Energy**—Of course, there is much more than pharmacology in Ayahuasca and other plant medicines. They possess wisdom teaching, astral and planetary knowledge, and deep energetic (physical and spiritual) healing properties. I cannot explain the essence as deeply as I would like. It must be experienced and I hope you will be called to work with Grandmother if you haven't yet.

Being in Circle with Grandmother Ayahuasca

I have been blessed with the opportunity to attend close to 20 Ayahuasca ceremonies so far in my life. Each one is unique in the nature of the colors and geometry I see, the insights from the cosmos, Gaia, and from those in circle with me. It's a very complex and deep journey with insights (downloads) that continue to come for weeks after being in a circle. The icaros sung by the Shipibo shamans and the space they hold weaves an additional higher dimensional field of energy within each participant. The icaros can also amplify the color, geometry, and imagery during the four to six hour session. It truly dances the medicine through your energy body. While the purge can be uncomfortable, there is definitely a deep clearing of negative energies that's appreciated, and an enhanced sense of spiritual, energetic, and physical well-being that is noted after each session. Some like to describe the benefits as analogous to peeling off layers of an onion to clear traumas, thus allowing yourself to purify and go deeper each time. One may experience various emotions and psychedelic states during a ceremony, including love, oneness, bliss, fear, forgiveness and so much more.

Back here at home, clinical research has delved into other potential therapeutic uses of Ayahuasca, including its effects on depression, PTSD, and addiction, though so much remains to be explored. At the recent MAPS (Multidisciplinary Association for Psychedelic Studies) Psychedelic Science Conference in Denver, I was impressed and encouraged after viewing several new studies at the poster session while also meeting the young, psychonaut researchers behind them! This much-needed research will provide the evidence needed for the scrutinizing scientific community and skeptics who remain on the fence in terms of therapeutic benefits, legalization or decriminalization.

Ayahuasca in the Sacred Valley of Peru

Many years ago, I traveled to Peru for my first Ayahuasca ceremony. I came not to simply see the famed and mysterious Machu Picchu, but more importantly, I aspired to make a significant leap in my spiritual awakening. I'd been feeling somewhat of a disconnect from my deeper self, nature, God, and the cosmos.

After the rigorous hike of the Inca Trail, followed by touring and connecting with the energies of Machu Picchu, I decided I needed to tap into higher dimensions with the help of a Shipibo shaman, who was offering Ayahuasca ceremonies near Pisac. Traditionally, he would perform these in the rainforest, but he'd been bringing the sacred brew upstream to another powerful mountainous region of Peru, known as the Sacred Valley. The main benefit is that it's a malaria-free zone with deep Inca ancestral energies to synergize with this plant medicine.

Prior to participating, I had to maintain a strict diet (dieta) for a few days, drinking only mineral water for the last 24 hours. The shaman also assisted me in making despacho, or offerings, to the Inca gods the afternoon before the ceremony. On this auspicious evening, I found myself in a circular thatched ceremony room in the Sacred Valley of Peru.

A fire burned in the center of the room and I found myself not in a large circle of 20, as often happens, but by myself—attended by one Shipibo shaman and a female apprentice. Personalized attention, for sure! The Shipibo's lineage, knowledge, medicine, and relationship with this plant made it the closest thing to being in the rainforest. His face was weathered, and I estimated him to be in his seventies. His eyes and energy field emanated wisdom and interdimensional connectedness. Despite feeling comfortable with his presence and grateful for the gift of individualized care, being alone without other Westerners had me feeling a bit uneasy.

At sunset, with the fire stoked in the center of the circular ceremonial room warming the cool room, I could hear the wind blowing down from the Apus of the Andes Mountains around us, rustling the thatched roof above us. A donkey hee-hawed in a nearby pasture. Wrapped in beautiful, bright-colored, geometrically patterned, llama-wool Peruvian blankets, I sat in fear on a meditation pillow.

Thoughts began to run through my head. *How crazy for me to do this! I could die or maybe flip out on this journey. This could change me forever.*

I centered myself and began a slow-breathing meditation to relax. I was told I had to trust in "Grandmother"—the medicine—and to speak my intention, but also allow her to do the needed work. It was similar to running off a cliff to paraglide. For a successful flight, you have to trust, let go, and flow with the whole process.

As the fire danced in front of my eyes, and the smoke snaked to the opening in the thatched roof, flowing to the stars on this clear, crisp night, the elder shaman began singing icaros to the medicine. The icaros are songs created by the Shipibo people of the Amazon to activate the maroon-colored medicine in the circle.

Soon he offered me a few ounces of Ayahuasca to drink. Swallowing quickly, I chased the bittersweet taste down with water and then waited in silence as more icaros were chanted to activate the medicine. First, the sound calmed the nausea from the medicine. For almost an hour, I sat listening and staring at the dancing flames, wondering if anything was going to happen. Suddenly, over minutes, I started seeing geometry—predominately hexagons—then three-dimensional shapes morphing into tetrahedrons and other complex forms beyond 3-D. The geometry came alive, with gold light intermixed with iridescent, fluorescent-like colors of unbelievable beauty.

At times multidimensional-seeming, it took me on a fractal trail that seemed to go to infinity. I felt a deep oneness with the universe. Then minuscule, segmented, snake-like forms appeared and traveled through my body, as if scanning my meridian lines. At one point, I could visualize them scanning through the double helix of my DNA—mending, then removing unwanted DNA fragments.

I journeyed into the other dimensions for a few hours—boosted even more deeply with an extra dose—visualizing things that would take another book to describe. A few times, the periodic intense waves of nausea almost made me throw up, but were calmed by the icaros; I held on a little longer. With my eyes closed, I noticed how the energy of the song intensified the geometry. When he stopped, the visual intensity of colors and geometry would drop off by at least one-third. Never had I imagined that sound would so profoundly increase the visual complexity and color saturation. This enhancement occurred with perfect synchrony to his chanting.

As the medicine and icaros continued their healing, I came to a distinct point where I knew it was time to cleanse and release what my physical, mental, and spiritual body no longer needed. Intense nausea hit me and I quickly grabbed the bucket beside me to purge. Anticipating I would simply see the plant medicine coming up, I was instead seeing a black hole-like vortex in the middle of the bucket. As the Ayahuasca was thrown up, I saw it funneling unwanted matter and negative energy into another dimension of outer space! I watched it circle up and out of the vortex just as water spirals down and out of a funnel, but instead this flowed up and out into the cosmos..

After this journey, I became convinced that plants, especially Ayahuasca, can favorably affect our DNA. In my case, in a cleansing of negative energies. Perhaps even clearing some mutations! Seeing the enhancement and increased complexity of geometry and color through music and chanting, I realized how—as we process these higher levels of light and geometry—sound can further stimulate our brain and likely our DNA. The out-of-body visualization of my energy field confirmed my belief in the Chinese acupuncture meridian system and the Ayurvedic chakra-based system.

Additional work with this sacred plant in Peru has produced similar experiences and greater insights. Everyone has been unique with varied intensities and diverse insights coming in each time. About a year later, I picked up Jeremy Narby's book, *The Cosmic Serpent, DNA and the Origins of Knowledge* (1998).[30] As an anthropologist, deep in the jungle with Amazonian Shipibo shamans, Narby studied the medicinal benefits of Ayahuasca.

To my surprise, Narby—eloquently and with great depth—describes the same fluorescent snakes I'd seen! He saw them as DNA-like—insightfully making the comparison: "DNA is the snake-shaped master of transformation that lives in water and is both extremely long and small, single and double. Just like the cosmic serpent . . . DNA is compared not only to two entwined serpents, but also precisely, to a rope, a vine, a ladder or a stairway."

As I looked at Jeremy's experience beside mine, the only difference was that the minute snakes were scanning and repairing my helical DNA, rather than actually being DNA.

In the classic shamanism book, "The Way of the Shaman: a Guide to Power and Healing" (1980)[31], Michael Harner describes how the majority of shamans he interviewed had seen, like him, colorful serpents. Harner documents the presence of the cosmic serpent—including: Ronin, the Amazonian two-headed anaconda; Quetzalcoatl, the Aztec feathered serpent; the Rainbow Snake of the Australian aborigines; the cosmic serpent of ancient Egyptians; the thousand-headed serpent god Sesha of the Hindus; and others. This intrigued me, as I'd been having dreams about Quetzalcoatl.

The plumed serpent Kukulkan is revered at the step pyramid (El Castillo) in Chichen Itza, where annually during the fall and spring equinox, watched by thousands, the shadow of the serpent appears on the side of the temple. I have visited this site a few times, and many other Mayan complexes since my college days.

The archaeoastronomical alignments that produce the undulating serpent shadow from Kulkulkan and other astral alignments are mind boggling. Even today's supercomputers with CAD architectural design integrating astronomical data and our modern construction techniques would struggle to construct a replica of pyramids in Yucatan, Mexico, and Egypt with the precision of the ancients. My travels to Peru, Bolivia, Easter Island, and Cambodia have stimulated even deeper curiosity and marvel of additional megalithic temple alignments. Sacred geometry is applied in most ancient temple constructions, which may include Phi ratios, Fibonacci sequences, squaring the circle, etc. The phi ratio (aka golden ratio) is found in the spiraling snake-like DNA double-stranded helix as well as the geometry of our Milky Way galaxy. "As above, so below."

In summary, Ayahuasca will heal and enlighten you. The journey isn't for lightweights, and don't expect it to be a spa-like retreat or party. As Grandmother and the shaman guide you to clear the darkness, bring in the light, and see what you need to change in your life, you will become stronger, bolder, more alive, and yes, a better lover.

Ayahuasca Summary

How It Works

- Ayahuasca contains the classic tryptamine psychedelic N,N-dimethyltryptamine (DMT) in combination with beta carboline or harmala alkaloid monoamine oxidase inhibitors (MAOIs).

- Use of harmala MAOIs that block MAO within the GI tract and liver are necessary for the oral use or bioavailability of DMT and subsequent production of psychedelic effects.

DMT

- DMT is a non-specific agonist at serotonin receptors: 5-HT1A/1B/1D, 5-HT2A/2B/2C, 5-HT5A, 5-HT6 and 5-HT7.

- DMT also interacts with glutamate receptors, Trace Amine Associated Receptor (TAAR) & σ-1 receptors as well as gene transcription factors.

References: 32,33,34,35.

Metabolism of Ayahuasca

Metabolism of DMT

- DMT is primarily metabolized by MAO-A, although may be metabolized via other metabolic routes, including aldehyde dehydrogenase, kynureninase, and other enzymes capable of N-oxidation.

- In combination with harmala MAOIs, the bioavailability, intensity of subjective effect, and duration of DMT's effects increase.

Metabolism of Harmala Alkaloids

- Harmine and harmaline can undergo metabolism by CYP2D6 and their systemic concentrations are sensitive to genetic variation of CYP2D6 phenotypes.

- Harmala alkaloids may be able to block CYP2D6, CYP3A4 as well as MAO-A.

  Reference: 36

Typical Dosing*

Standard dose serving of Ayahuasca for a 75kg (165lb) adult contains approximately:

- 0.5-1 mg/kg DMT = 37.5-75mg DMT
- 60-125 mg harmine
- 4-9 mg harmaline
- 50-100 mg tetrahydroharmine (THH)

  *Strength and contents of Ayahuasca brews can vary considerably. Typical doses of liquid Ayahuasca range between five to 45 ml.

Common Journey Experiences

- Ayahuasca is notorious for heavy or purgative somatic effects such as nausea, vomiting, GI upset, or diarrhea.

- DMT often produces intense hallucinations and a sense of another being or entity being present.

- Onset of effects ~15 to 60 minutes, peak effects 45 to 120 minutes, total duration of effects three to six hours.

Potential Therapeutic Uses

The complex botanical nature, use of MAOIs, and heavy somatic "side effects" of Ayahuasca have limited interest in conducting clinical trials, however, small and positive studies exist for the treatment of refractory depression as well as substance use disorders. There are likely several therapeutic uses, purposes, or indications for this sacrament. It's unlikely Ayahuasca is referred to as "the medicine" due to lack of therapeutic application.

- Treatment-resistant unipolar depression.
- Substance Use Disorders.

Potential Adverse Effects

Physical

Nausea, vomiting
Increased blood pressure & heart rate
Discomfort

Psych/Neuro

Transient anxiety
Emotional discomfort
Paranoia or confusion

Potential Drug Interactions & Contraindications

Drug Interactions

The mechanism of Ayahuasca itself is dependent upon the drug interaction of MAOI harmala alkaloids and DMT. The use of MAOIs in Ayahuasca carries special significance when considering drug interaction potential. The use of other drugs or medications that can boost monoamine (5HT, NE, DA) neurotransmission carry dangers of extreme adverse reactions such as serotonin toxicity, hypertensive crisis, seizures, or death. The following is a list of substances currently known to carry clinically significant drug interaction potential with MAOIs and be contraindicated with Ayahuasca. Times of avoidance prior to safe use of Ayahuasca vary by drug listed. There may be other medications or supplements of concern:

- Antidepressants (SSRI, SNRI, clomipramine, imipramine)
- Lithium
- Ziprasidone
- Amphetamine, methamphetamine
- Methylphenidate
- Cocaine
- St. John's Wort

- Dextromethorphan (Robitussin)
- Pseudoephedrine (Sudafed)
- Chlorpheniramine
- Phentermine (Adipex)
- Ephedra (Ma Huang)
- Methadone
- Tramadol
- Meperidine
- Tapentadol
- Ergotamine
- Phenethylamines—MDMA, 2Cx, DOx, NBOMe
- Tryptamines— 5-MeO-DMT
- Cathinones—Mephedrone, methylone, MPDV
- Purgative Sacraments—Kambo, Systemic (PO/PR) tobacco cleanses

Drug interaction studies between DMT and many other substances are lacking at this time, although are likely similar to drug interactions with psilocybin/psilocin:

- Lithium → Increased risk of seizures or dysphoric experience quality, contraindicated.
- ChronicLong-term (4+ weeks) of SSRI/SNRI or MAOI use → Possible diminished effects.
- Buspirone → Possible diminished effects.
- Acute MAOI use (necessary for Ayahuasca) → Intensified psychedelic effects.

- Benzodiazepines → Possible diminished effects.

- Atypical antipsychotics → Reduced psychedelic effects.

- Triptan migraine agents → Vasoconstriction and increased cardiovascular risks.

Contraindicated

- Bipolar I or severe bipolar conditions.

- Schizophrenia, psychosis, or psychotic conditions.

- Hereditary fructose intolerance (Ayahuasca is high in fructose).

Legality

Ayahuasca contains dimethyltryptamine (DMT), which is classified as a Schedule I controlled substance under federal law. This means that DMT is illegal to possess, distribute, or use for recreational purposes at the federal level. However, there are no legal restrictions on harmala alkaloids.

- Several religious groups, such as the Santo Daime and the União do Vegetal (UDV), have successfully argued that their sacramental use of Ayahuasca is protected under the RFRA, which grants exemptions for religious practices that involve controlled substances like DMT.

- The legal status of Ayahuasca for religious purposes is not uniform across the United States.

- The importation, distribution, and sale of Ayahuasca can still be subject to prosecution under federal drug laws.

Chapter 11

DMT: The Oneness Molecule

DMT (N,N-Dimethyltryptamine) is a potent classic psychedelic tryptamine that can induce intense and profound experiences. These experiences can vary widely from person to person and can include mystical, spiritual, and deeply introspective elements. However, DMT is commonly known as the "Spirit Molecule," due to a characteristic interactive relational experience that occurs at high doses. While many other psychedelics can shift a person towards complete non-duality (mystical experiences of unity with all things), DMT tends to preserve duality and engender encounters with entities, spirits, beings, deities, or aliens.

For a great overview of DMT, please read Rick Straussman's book, *DMT: The Spirit Molecule*.[37] DMT is found widely throughout different plants and animals. It also acts as an endogenous neurotransmitter in humans. However, only a few plants contain DMT in high enough concentrations to warrant extraction from them. Below are the most common forms of DMT.

Forms of DMT, Natural and Synthetic

- The most common form of DMT—N,N-Dimethyltryptamine—is a crystalline powder, which can range in color from white to yellowish. This form is typically vaporized or smoked, often in a pipe or specially designed vaporizer. The effects are rapid and intense, usually lasting between five to 30 minutes. It can be isolated from particular plants and a toad.

- Ayahuasca: As discussed earlier, this plant medicine naturally contains DMT, and is blended with an MAOI-containing plant like Banisteriopsis caapi. The MAOI prevents the breakdown of DMT in the digestive system, allowing it to enter the bloodstream and cross the blood-brain barrier.

- 5-MeO-DMT: While chemically related to DMT, 5-MeO-DMT is a distinct compound found in certain plants and the venom of the Bufo alvarius toad. It's known for its powerful, fast-acting psychedelic effects, which are often described as more introspective and less visually intense than those of DMT.

This form can also be vaporized or smoked and has a short duration of effects.

- Changa: A smokable blend of herbs infused with DMT. It often includes an MAOI-containing plant, which can alter and prolong the effects of the DMT.

- The experience of smoking Changa can be milder and longer than smoking pure crystalline DMT, with the duration of effects typically ranging from 10 to 20 minutes.

- Yopo or Anadenanthera: A traditional snuff prepared from the beans of the Anadenanthera Peregrina tree, which is Indigenous to the Caribbean and South America. The beans are rich in DMT and are sometimes mixed with lime or other additives to make them active when insufflated.

- Virola Snuff: This is another type of snuff made from the resin of the Virola tree. The snuff, which contains DMT and other related tryptamines, is used by various Indigenous groups in South America for shamanic purposes.

- Other DMT-Containing Plants include: Mimosa hostilis/root bark aka Jurema, and Acacia confusa, which contain DMT. These plants are used either in traditional brews like Ayahuasca or are processed to extract pure DMT.

- Pharmahuasca: This is a modern, synthetic version of Ayahuasca, made by combining pure DMT with a pharmaceutical MAOI. For example, moclobemide is a reversible inhibitor of MAO-A, which is similar to the mechanism of harmala alkaloids. Harmala alkaloids can also be sourced from Syrian Rue, as opposed to Banisteriopisis Caapi.

The experience is similar to Ayahuasca, but can be more easily controlled in terms of dosage and composition. Of course, this synthetic version will not contain the shamanic essence or energy of natural Ayahuasca.[38,39,40]

Inhaled DMT

The inhaled DMT experience and Ayahuasca are likely the most popular modalities today. Of course, I can't find a survey or accurate data to confirm that, but based on the psychedelic community's informal feedback, that seems to be the case. The duration of inhaled DMT is much shorter than Ayahuasca and lasts ~eight to 20 minutes as opposed to four to six hours. When used via inhalation, many people focus on "breakthrough" experiences, which tend to reliably produce interactive-relational experiences. However, DMT can be used in smaller doses for purposes of healing, connection, or therapeutic effects.

One important difference between DMT and other classic tryptamines like psilocybin/psilocin is the lack of apparent tolerance to subjective effects with repeated dosing. To this end, persons may find a great degree of safety, titratability, control, and benefit when using DMT formulated in a vapor pen. Finding vapor pens can be challenging, though, and if so desired, one should find a trusted underground chemist or pharmacist who makes them in a safe base.

DMT Journey Experiences:

The experience of a DMT journey can be highly individual and unpredictable, ranging from intense fractal visuals to white light in a vacuum of space, to expansions into oneness. For me, I often rocket into the white light, then descend into the fractal visions on 5-Meo-DMT. Naturally, they have the potential to enhance connections between individuals, including lovers, in several ways:

- Shared Experience: When romantic partners choose to embark on a DMT journey together, they may share a deeply transformative and mystical experience. This shared experience can create a strong sense of connection and unity. Unless a third party serves them, they would need to serve and hold space for the other, as high-dose simultaneous journeying is not recommended. We have found that enjoying a few hits by vape of N,N, DMT can open us up to a mystical and deep sacred sexual connection. Our passion is often ignited with this molecule, but the duration is short, typically just 20-30 minutes requiring repeat doses. Geometry and portals can open up with higher doses, allowing for meditative moments of oneness together.

- Enhanced Communication: DMT experiences often involve altered states of consciousness and may lead to a heightened sense of empathy and understanding. Partners may find it easier to communicate openly and honestly about their feelings, desires, and experiences, deepening their emotional connection.

- Emotional Bonding: The intensity and profundity of a DMT journey can lead to a sense of emotional bonding between individuals. This can result in a deeper emotional connection and a sense of shared growth and exploration.

- Transcendence of Ego: DMT journeys can dissolve the boundaries of the ego, allowing individuals to experience a sense of oneness with the universe. This transcendence of ego can lead to a feeling of interconnectedness with others, fostering a sense of unity and love. The ultimate again is merging into oneness with your partner and the universe around you.

- Enhanced Sensory Perception: DMT can profoundly affect sensory perception, leading to heightened awareness and sensory experiences. This enhanced perception can lead to a greater appreciation of the sensory aspects of love and physical connection. I've been able to feel and balance my chakras with my own hands towards the tail end of a DMT journey. Learning how to do energy work on yourself and others can give you more opportunities for deeper healing with DMT. Sexually, most couples will feel enhanced sensitivity after a DMT journey, as well as more profound orgasms.

- Reflection and Integration: After a DMT journey, individuals often reflect on their experiences and attempt to integrate the insights gained into their daily lives. Partners can support each other in this integration process, which can lead to personal and relational growth. Journaling can be especially helpful, and support via a therapist is recommended if you need assistance with challenging issues.

Please note that DMT is a Schedule I controlled substance in many countries, including the United States, and its use is illegal except for certain religious groups who have been granted exemptions (e.g., some Ayahuasca-using churches). Despite its potential for spiritual experiences, DMT can also pose psychological and physiological risks, especially when used without proper guidance or in an unsafe context. As mentioned, it can be sourced from different plants and the Bufo toad, so be aware of your impacts and use sustainable and safely procured and tested psychedelics.

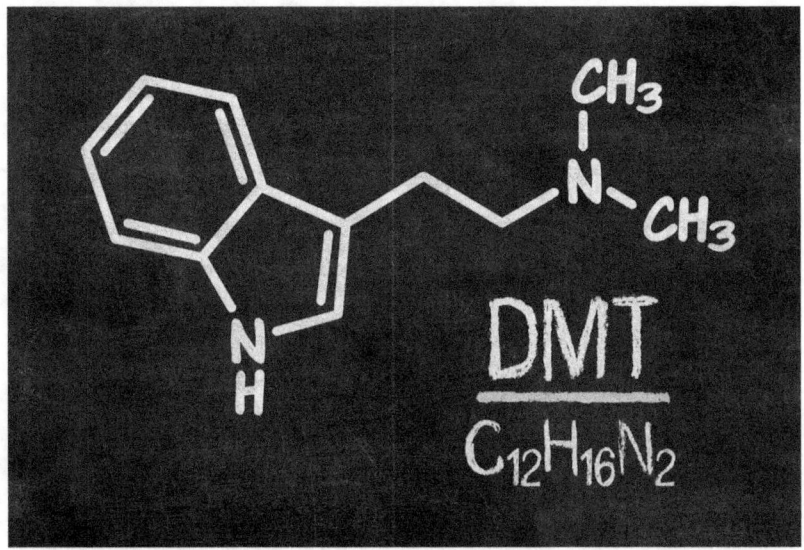

N,N-dimethyltryptamine (DMT)

How It Works

DMT Summary

- DMT is a non-specific agonist at serotonin receptors: 5-HT1A/1B/1D, 5-HT2A/2B/2C, 5-HT5A, 5-HT6 and 5-HT7.

- DMT also interacts with glutamate receptors, Trace Amine Associated Receptor (TAAR) & σ-1 receptors as well as gene transcription factors.

Metabolism of DMT

- DMT is primarily metabolized by MAO-A, although may be metabolized via other metabolic routes, including aldehyde dehydrogenase, kynureninase, and other enzymes capable of N-oxidation.

- In combination with harmala MAOIs, the bioavailability, intensity of subjective effect, and duration of DMT's effects increase.

Typical Dosing*

- Threshold: 1-3 mg
- Low: 4-10 mg
- Moderate: 10-30 mg
- High: >30 mg

  *Based on use via inhalation route via an efficient device (e.g., Mighty vaporizer) it is possible to achieve a "breakthrough" dose of DMT with as little as 30 mg. However, less efficient devices or less sensitive persons may need 50 to 100 mg to achieve a "breakthrough" dose. This information is not to be construed as suggesting "breakthrough" doses are the goal or necessary for healing effects or greater communion with your partner.

Common Journey Experiences

- DMT often produces intense hallucinations and a sense of another being or entity being present.

- As inhaled DMT w/o MAOIs: Onset of effects <10 seconds; peak effects two to five minutes; total experience duration 10 to 20 minutes.

Potential Therapeutic Uses

- Treatment-resistant unipolar depression.

Potential Adverse Effects

Physical

Nausea, vomiting
Increased blood pressure & heart rate
Discomfort

Psych/Neuro

Transient anxiety
Emotional discomfort
Paranoia or confusion
Tinnitus

Potential Drug Interactions & Contraindications

Drug Interactions

Drug interaction studies between DMT and many other substances are lacking at this time, although are likely similar to drug interactions with psilocybin/psilocin:

- Lithium → Increased risk of seizures or dysphoric experience quality, contraindicated.

- ChronicLong-term (four+ weeks) of SSRI/SNRI or MAOI use → Possible diminished effects.

- Buspirone → Possible diminished effects.

- Acute MAOI use (necessary for Ayahuasca) → Intensified psychedelic effects.

- Benzodiazepines → Possible diminished effects.

- Atypical antipsychotics → Reduced psychedelic effects.

- Triptan migraine agents → Vasoconstriction and increased cardiovascular risks.

Contraindicated

- Bipolar I or severe bipolar conditions.

- Schizophrenia, psychosis, or psychotic conditions.

Legality

DMT (N,N-Dimethyltryptamine) is classified as a Schedule I controlled substance under federal law. This means that DMT is illegal to manufacture, possess, distribute, or use for recreational or non-medical purposes at the federal level.

- Some research institutions and scientists may be authorized to use DMT for research purposes, provided they have the necessary permits and approvals.

Chapter 12

Catalysts to Boost and Enhance a Psychedelic Journey

Over the last few years, I've been safely experimenting with combinations of various plant medicines to appreciate how one can potentiate or amplify an ongoing psychedelic journey. Please recognize that combining plant medicines should only be considered in those with extensive psychedelic experience for the most part. An example of this would be the Nexus Flip (MDMA/2-CB) discussed earlier. Applying other plant medicines to an ongoing plant medicine journey can be done towards the end of the journey to prolong the duration, add extra stimulation, or enhance ongoing, heart-opening empathogenic properties. On the flip side, certain ones can be used to help cool off individuals who are overstimulated from a psychedelic. CBD is the best and safest go-to for this. Sometimes falling asleep after a long day with San Pedro and other plant medicines can be a challenge, too, so one could consider a small amount of Indica, CBD, and melatonin to address this.

Here are a few of my favorites worth mentioning:

Rapeh—also known as Rape' Hape', Hapi, or snuff, is an herbal powdered mixture that combines tobacco, tree bark, and medicinal plants. This traditional snuff has been used by Indigenous South American tribes for generations and holds great cultural significance. It plays a prominent role in shamanic practices, particularly in Ayahuasca ceremonies, and is also used independently for its medicinal and healing properties.

I initially tried this shamanic medicine a long time ago during an Ayahuasca ceremony and found it way too intense. Looking back at the experience, I think the shaman's assistant probably gave me three times what I needed! I tried it again a couple of years ago at a lower dose and now love it! Truly a magical plant medicine with a variety of blends to choose from, depending on where you want to travel. Some blends offer more of a grounding effect, and others are more astral in nature. So if you are feeling off the planet already, the last thing you want to do is a Rapeh blend that contains DMT compounds. Seek the more grounding blends, some of which are mentioned below.

The administration of Rapeh involves blowing the mixture into the nostrils using a tube called a Tepi, which can be done by a shaman or a trusted friend. Alternatively, one can use a Kuripe to self-administer the snuff. As always, it's best to learn this technique from an experienced facilitator or shaman before trying it yourself. It's not as easy as it sounds.

The primary active ingredient in Rapeh is nicotine (from tobacco powder), which stimulates the release of dopamine, norepinephrine, and acetylcholine. When combined with the other medicinal ingredients, it produces sensations of euphoria, pleasure, reward, and motivation. Certain formulations of Rapeh may contain harmala alkaloids, which act as MAO inhibitors, elevating serotonin and other neurotransmitters.

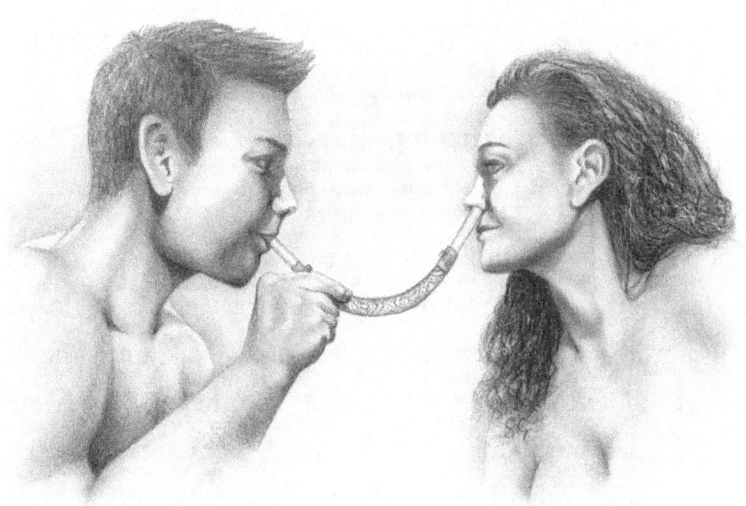

Rapeh is blown through a Tepi into Bella's nose.

When a dose of Rapeh powder is blown into the nose, it induces a burning sensation in the upper nasal passages, causing the eyes to water and the nose to run for approximately five to 10 minutes. It is common to experience dizziness and instability on one's feet, so it's advisable to remain seated in a safe location during the experience. Purging can happen more rarely and is usually due to a high dose. If you're sensitive to Rapeh like me, start low, then you can always go up on subsequent doses.

Rapeh can enhance sacred sexual flow and libido, in my opinion. This is most likely due to the dopamine-boosting effects. I use a balanced blend like Yawanawá that gives Bella and me a reasonable amount of grounding with beautiful expansion of energies into the crown chakra and third eye. Every Rapeh blend I have tried also has a heart-opening effect, and I typically feel my pulse rate increase by 20 to 30 from baseline.

Third-Eye Connecting with Rapeh: Begin by facing your lover and holding hands while engaging in a few minutes of eye gazing. Set intentions before beginning. This can be as simple as, "I want to flow to a space of deeper love with you."

Decide on who would like to go first. Administer the rapeh up each nostril to your lover, and then if the receiver is capable, have them administer yours. If they're too dizzy, wait until they are more grounded before giving to you. Another good option is to puff Rapeh into your partner's nostrils with a Tepi and then self-administer with a Kuripe. The goal is to be dropped in close to the same time after you have had some experience going one at a time. Touching your foreheads and aligning the "third eye" chakras can foster an intimate connection between partners.

Doing so, you should feel an increased tingling sensation as your third eyes connect. Breathe into this together and flow into an ecstatic euphoric state together, while at the same time feeling yourself staying grounded with your root chakras. Another favorite technique is for me to breathe into Bella as she inhales, and vice-versa. This is deeply intimate, especially on Rapeh.

This medicine can serve as an entry point to foreplay, a midpoint, or as a finale after making love. If desired, individuals can enjoy one to three rounds of Rapeh, but it is recommended to space them apart by at least 30 minutes.

Third Eye Connecting after Rapeh.

Here are the common Rapeh (Rapé) blends to consider:

- Yawanawá Rapé: Made by the Yawanawá tribe, this blend is known for its powerful effects and is often used for profound spiritual journeying.

- Nukini Rapé: Created by the Nukini tribe, it's famed for its gentle, healing properties, often used for emotional and physical healing.

- Kaxinawá (Huni Kuin) Rapé: Prepared by the Kaxinawá tribe, this rapé is used in spiritual ceremonies and is known for its strong effects and connection to tribal ancestors.

- Katukina Rapé: The Katukina tribe makes this blend, which is often used for clarity, focus, and deepening one's connection to the natural world.

- Matsés (Mayoruna) Rapé: Made by the Matsés tribe, it is known for its intense effects and is traditionally used for hunting, enhancing senses, and focus.

- Puyanawa Rapé: This blend, crafted by the Puyanawa tribe, is often used in social settings for its uplifting and energizing effects.

- Tsunu Rapé: Known for its grounding and center-ing qualities, Tsunu rapé often includes ash from the Tsunu tree and is used in various ceremonies.

- Muru Muru Rapé: Often used for meditation and grounding, this blend includes the ash of the Muru Muru tree and is known for its calming properties.

- Yopo or Anadenanthera: Yopo is a traditional snuff pre-pared from the beans of the Anadenanthera Peregrina tree, which is Indigenous to the Caribbean and South America. The beans are rich in DMT and are some-times mixed with lime or other additives to make them active when insufflated. This one can really take you astral.

- Virola Snuff: This is another type of snuff made from the resin of the Virola tree. The snuff, which contains DMT and other related tryptamines, is used by various Indigenous groups in South America for shamanic purposes.

Rapeh, like other plant medicines, should be held in a sacred container of respect and mindfulness, recognizing its cultural significance, healing, and enlightening effects on the mind and body. It's always best to seek guidance from an experienced practitioner or friend to learn the most beneficial and safe ways to work with this medicine.

In addition to using Rapeh with Ayahuasca, I've found it to extend and potentiate the effects of psilocybin, THC, LSD, and others. A low dose of a rapeh blend that is balanced and without a profound astral effect is important when combined with other psychedelics. It is always best to wait until the primary psychedelic has already peaked and the effects have lightened significantly.

Blue Lotus Herb

Also known as Nyphaea Caerulea or Blue Water Lily, this is a remarkable herb known for its numerous benefits in the realm of sacred sexuality and for enhanced sense of overall well-being.

In ancient Egyptian times, it was commonly consumed as a tea for its aphrodisiac properties, but it also offered various other advantages, such as mood elevation, stress reduction, and enhanced blood flow to the genital area.

For those interested in exploring Blue Lotus further, one can find many tinctures and dried flowers online. To prepare a tea using dried Blue Lotus flowers, begin with one to two grams and allow it to steep for approximately 20 minutes before consumption. If desired, honey can be added for additional sweetness. It's important to note that the optimal dosage may vary, as with other plant medicines, so some experimentation may be necessary. Seeking guidance from an herbalist can provide further insight, personalized advice, and the option to blend in other synergistic herbs.

Another great option is to grind one gram of the herb up and blend it with one gram of ground psilocybin before using the Lemon Tek extraction technique. Lemon tekking can increase the potency, so use a lower dose of psilocybin than usual. (To learn the technique see: https://thethirdwave.co/lemon-tekking-shrooms/.) This can then be served as a tea and sweetened with honey. Enjoy!!

Blue Lotus is thought to contain compounds that can have mild psychoactive effects, although it is not as potent as some other psychoactive substances.

The primary pharmacologically active constituents in Blue Lotus are believed to be:

- Aporphine: A compound that is a non-selective dopamine agonist and can lead to a sense of euphoria and has psychoactive effects.

- Nuciferine: An alkaloid that is thought to be a dopamine receptor antagonist with potential sedative and relaxing effects.

The effects of Blue Lotus are generally described as mild and can include a sense of relaxation, mild sedation, euphoria, and altered consciousness. People who use the Blue Lotus report it can help to relieve stress, enhance mood, increase feelings of well-being, and provide a slight feeling of being "high." Most importantly, it should help enhance libido and sexual flow, due to its aphrodisiac properties.

To complement the tea experience, Blue Lotus is also available as an aromatherapy option. Bring this scent into your bedroom for an olfactory stimulation in addition to the tea, or with other plant medicines. Blue Lotus can also be paired well with other psychedelics.

THC

Tetrahydrocannabinol (THC) can be an adjunct to most psychedelic molecules. One must be cautious of course, and it's best to add in after one has passed the peak of the primary psychedelic. Smoking or vaping is safest, so you don't overdo it and fall into a dissociated or paranoid state. Indica, of course, can help calm the experience, and Sativa better if you need more stimulation. Oftentimes it will bring back psychedelic colors and imagery that may be tapering off as psilocybin and other plant medicines are clearing your body.

CBD

Cannabidiol is one of the numerous compounds found in the Cannabis plant that has many potential therapeutic effects, without the psychoactive effects typically associated with tetrahydrocannabinol (THC), another well-known cannabinoid. It can be a beneficial add-on to a psychedelic journey to help reduce nausea, in addition to ginger. Other benefits include:

- Reducing anxiety. This can be helpful if overstimulated during a psychedelic journey. Magnesium threonate can also help. I use CBD, melatonin, and Magnesium threonate combined to help with sleep after intense journeys.

- Neuroprotective and anti-inflammatory. For this reason, it can be helpful at the end of an MDMA journey. It may help reduce inflammation systemically, and it is being studied in various conditions associated with inflammation.

- Reduction in nausea and vomiting, which can be beneficial for individuals who get nauseated from psychedelics.

How does it work?

As discussed earlier, CBD acts through various mechanisms of action. It interacts with cannabinoid receptors in the endocannabinoid system, but also affects other receptors such as serotonin (5-HT1A), vanilloid, and adenosine receptors. Additionally, CBD can modulate the activity of various ion channels and non-cannabinoid receptors, which helps explain its broad range of potential therapeutic effects. The efficacy and safety profile of CBD can vary depending on the dose, formulation, and presence of other cannabinoids. Full-spectrum CBD products, which contain a range of cannabinoids and terpenes, may have different effects compared to CBD isolate due to the "entourage effect," a theory suggesting that cannabinoids have greater therapeutic potential when used together.

It's also important to note that while CBD is generally well-tolerated, it can cause side effects in some people and may interact with certain medications. Start low at 10 to 20 mg by tincture and repeat the dose in an hour, if needed.

Tongkat Ali

Also known as Eurycoma longifolia, this herbal plant is native to Southeast Asian countries. It's often used in traditional medicine, particularly in Indonesia, Malaysia, and Vietnam. The root of the plant is where most of the bioactive compounds are found, and it's this part of the plant that's commonly used in supplements.

Regarding sexual performance, Tongkat Ali is reputed to have several potential benefits:

- Increased Testosterone Levels: Some studies suggest that this herb may increase testosterone levels in men with low levels, thus enhancing libido and erectile function.

- Libido Enhancement is often seen for both men and women.

- Erectile Function is likely improved with this herb, although more research is needed to confirm this.

- Adrenal balancing by its ability to reduce cortisol levels (stress hormone).

- Dosing is typically 200 to 400 mg of a standardized extract per day. This extract is typically standardized to a certain percentage of eurycomanone, the active compound.

Cacao

Cacao, from which chocolate is made, originally comes from the Amazon basin. It's believed to have been first cultivated by the Olmecs in Mexico as early as 1500 BC, and later by the Mayans and Aztecs. The cacao tree, Theobroma cacao, thrives in the tropical climates of Central and South America, and its use has a long and rich history in these regions.

Cacao (or cocoa) contains compounds that can have subtle effects on mood and physiological processes, which may indirectly influence libido for some individuals. While cacao itself is not typically considered an aphrodisiac in the traditional sense, there are a few ways in which it might contribute to an increased sense of well-being, enhanced libido, and improved sacred sexual flow. These include:

- Mood Enhancement: Cacao contains compounds such as theobromine, caffeine, and phenylethylamine (PEA), which can have mild mood-enhancing and stimulant effects. These compounds may contribute to feelings of alertness, energy, and general well-being, which could indirectly enhance libido by putting individuals in a more positive mood.

- Relaxation: Cacao also contains serotonin precursors, which can promote relaxation and a sense of contentment. Reduced stress and anxiety levels can be beneficial for sexual desire and performance.

- Vasodilation: Some studies suggest that the flavonoids found in dark chocolate (which is derived from cacao) may promote improved blood flow and circulation.

Enhanced blood flow to genital areas can increase sexual responsiveness.

- Sensory Pleasure: The taste and texture of chocolate and cacao can be pleasurable for many people, and the sensory experience of consuming chocolate or cocoa-based products can contribute to a positive mood and sense of enjoyment, potentially enhancing sexual experiences.

- Effects of cacao on libido can vary widely from person to person, as with every plant medicine. While some individuals may report feeling more sensual or amorous after consuming cacao, others may feel subtle to no effect.

Muira Puama

Scientifically known as Ptychopetalum olacoides, this bush is native to the Brazilian Amazon. Traditionally used in South American herbal medicine, it's often referred to as "potency wood." Muira Puama is reputed for its various therapeutic properties, and it's used for a range of health conditions. Here are some of its notable properties:

- Aphrodisiac Effects: Muira Puama is famous for its reputation as a natural aphrodisiac. It's traditionally used to increase libido and sexual desire in both men and women, although scientific evidence supporting these effects is limited.

- Erectile Dysfunction: It is often used to treat erectile dysfunction, with some traditional use and preliminary studies suggesting it might help improve sexual function, but more research is needed to confirm these effects.

- Neuroprotective Properties: Some studies suggest that Muira Puama may have neuroprotective properties, potentially beneficial in conditions like Alzheimer's disease, though much of this research is in the early stages.

Typical dosing: For standardized extracts in capsule or tablet form, take a dose of 300 to 500 milligrams taken one to two times daily. It is also available in tea form, and tinctures.

Horny Goat Weed

Baaa. Horny Goat Weed, also known as Epimedium, is a herb that has been used in traditional Chinese medicine for centuries. It is reputed for various health benefits, particularly in the areas of sexual function and bone health. Here are some of its notable properties:

- Improvement in Erectile Dysfunction: Horny Goat Weed contains icariin, a compound that is thought to work by increasing nitric oxide levels, which relaxes muscle tissue and may help increase blood flow to the penis, potentially improving erectile function.

- Libido Enhancement: Has been traditionally used as an aphrodisiac to boost libido in both men and women. However, scientific evidence to support this effect is limited.

- Anti-Inflammatory Properties: Animal studies have indicated that Horny Goat Weed might have anti-inflammatory effects, which could be beneficial for conditions like arthritis, though more research is needed in humans.

- Neuroprotective Effects: There is some preliminary evidence to suggest that icariin, the active compound in Horny Goat Weed, may have neuroprotective effects, potentially beneficial in neurodegenerative diseases.

Typical capsule dosing is 250 mg to 1000 mg, taken once or twice daily.

Damiana

Scientifically known as Turnera diffusa, this small shrub is native to the southern United States, Central America, Mexico, South America, and the Caribbean. It has been used traditionally as an herbal remedy and is known for its various properties. Here are some notable characteristics and purported benefits of Damiana:

- Aphrodisiac enhancement: It's most famous for its reputation as a natural aphrodisiac. It's traditionally been used to increase sexual desire and performance, although scientific evidence is limited.

- Mood Enhancement: Some people use Damiana for its mood-lifting and anti-anxiety effects.

- Digestive Health: Can be used to treat digestive issues and is believed to act as a mild laxative and can help relieve constipation and improve gastrointestinal function.

- Energy Boost and Stimulant: Some users report that Damiana acts as a mild stimulant, providing a boost in energy levels. This may be partly due to its caffeine-like compounds.

- Antioxidant Properties: Like many herbs, Damiana contains natural antioxidants, which help neutralize harmful free radicals in the body.

Last But Not least, Peptides! Oxytocin and PT-141

Oxytocin

Oxytocin, often dubbed the "love hormone," is a peptide hormone and neuropeptide that plays a significant role in social bonding and sexual reproduction. It's produced in the hypothalamus and released by the pituitary gland. Please don't confuse this with the narcotic oxycontin.

From a sexual standpoint, oxytocin has some amazing benefits:

- Enhancing Social Bonding: It's released during sexual activity, and it's believed to help strengthen the bond between partners. This bonding effect is seen as crucial in long-term relationships.

- Increasing Sexual Arousal: There is evidence to suggest that oxytocin can increase sexual arousal. It may heighten the sense of intimacy and connection, which can be an important component of sexual desire.

- Facilitating Orgasm: Oxytocin levels typically increase during sexual arousal and peak at orgasm. The hormone is thought to contribute to the intensity and satisfaction of the orgasmic experience for women and men. Part of this happens due to the enhanced smooth muscle contractions during orgasm for women in the vagina for women and prostate for men. Nipple orgasms for gals are much easier and more intense with this peptide, too! By augmenting your natural production, wild things will happen!

- Stress reduction: The release helps reduce anxiety and promote deep relaxation.

Typical dosing: 40 units by nasal spray prescribed by your physician and filled by a compounding pharmacy. It can also be compounded into sublingual troches, or rectal suppositories, based on your preference. Most physicians won't know how to prescribe this unless they specialize in hormone replacement, sexual health, and/or Functional Medicine. Compounded medications like this won't be covered by your insurance, but you might be able to use your health savings account. This is one of our favorites!

PT-141

PT-141, also known as Bremelanotide, is a synthetic peptide developed for its potential benefits in sexual health. It's the first medication approved by the FDA for the treatment of Hypoactive Sexual Desire Disorder (HSDD) in premenopausal women. Unlike other sexual dysfunction drugs that primarily work by affecting blood flow, PT-141 works on the nervous system. Here are some of the key aspects and benefits of PT-141:

- Mechanism of Action: PT-141 is a melanocortin receptor agonist. It acts on the central nervous system by activating the melanocortin receptors involved in sexual arousal and desire. It makes you crazy horny, basically. This mechanism is different from drugs like Viagra, which work by increasing blood flow to the genitals.

- For women, it's approved for treating hypoactive sexual desire disorder (HSDD), which is characterized by a lack of sexual desire causing marked distress or interpersonal difficulty. Clinical trials have shown that PT-141 can be effective in increasing sexual desire in women, which can last up to 24 hours.

- For men, while it's not FDA-approved for treating erectile dysfunction, some studies have shown that it can help in increasing sexual desire and may assist in achieving erections, especially in cases where other treatments are ineffective. I have tried it twice for field research and found it to produce an erection for hours. Most patients I've treated have had amazing results, but the doses may need to be adjusted up some to achieve optimal effect. Effectiveness: Most men and women report experiencing increased sexual desire within hours of taking the medication, and the effects can last up to 24 hours.

Administration: PT-141 is best administered via a subcutaneous injection with a tiny insulin syringe in abdomen fat, or by a nasal spray. If going subcutaneous, start low at ½ mg and inject in belly fat three to four hours prior to intercourse. Your physician and pharmacist can guide you on how much to pull up in an insulin syringe that equates to this amount. This, too, must be prescribed by a physician who has expertise in sexual health. Typically it's made in a compounding pharmacy and not covered by insurance. In general, anything for health and wellness is not covered by insurance.

Chapter 13

Up and Coming Developments in Psychedelics!

Grass-Roots Developments

Recently I attended the "Psychedelic Cup" sponsored by the non-profit Psychedelic Club of Denver. I'm just a spectator and love hanging out with this weird and eclectic group of people! Growers of various psilocybin mushroom species competed by submitting their home-grown samples for laboratory analysis of psilocin content prior to the event. Prizes were awarded to the top three, including the one with the lowest psilocin content. Detailed HPLC (High Performance LIquid Chromatography) analysis of the top samples were displayed on a big screen for geeks like myself to salivate over. Community events like this demonstrate how there's amazing ongoing "homegrown" R&D supported by non-profit psychedelic clubs to further progress the quality and efficacy of psychedelic therapies. Being in a community with this passionate group of individuals that's more focused on collective good, rather than profit, gives me hope as this movement accelerates.

The organic growth of psychedelic clubs across the country offers hope for further collaborations amongst clubs across the nation. Opportunities to educate members on how to grow mushrooms, reduce potential harm, and to share psychedelic journey tips serves this community well.

Various individuals and groups are stepping up to help psychonauts of all levels to prepare and fine-tune protocols for safe journeys/harm reduction.

Spirit Pharmacist, Ben Malcolm PharmD (Board Certified Psychiatric Pharmacist), offers comprehensive psychedelic educational programs as well as consultations for individuals who may be on psychiatric medications that need to safely taper off before engaging in Ayahuasca journeys, etc. For a reasonable consultation fee, he can safely guide you. Learn more at: https://www. spiritpharmacist.com/site/about. He helped compose all of the amazing summary charts in this book.

The Fireside Project is a non-profit group offering an important safety net for those having a difficult trip. This can happen to any of us, regardless of experience. Volunteers take calls from individuals who are struggling, while allowing you to maintain anonymity, as they help you relax and come down from a disorienting or tough journey with psychedelics. This also helps prevent many unneeded visits to the ER. Visit: https://firesideproject.org/ and please consider donating to their cause.

Last, but not least, there are several groups working to support Indigenous tribes around the world for the sustainable, respectable use of plant medicines. These include non-profits such as the Indigenous Reciprocity Initiative of the Americas (IRI), Riverstyx Foundation, Indigenous Peyote Conservation Initiative, Indigenous Medicine Conservation Fund, and the Chacruna

Institute for Psychedelic Plant Medicines. Please consider supporting one of these non-profits as well. I am hopeful that these non-profits will not silo themselves and instead seek to collaborate and synergize their efforts in the spirit of plant medicine and oneness as they support the Indigenous communities.

Psychedelics for the Treatment of Addiction Disorders—Iboga/Ibogaine

Ibogaine is a naturally occurring psychoactive substance found in plants in the Apocynaceae family, such as Tabernanthe iboga, a shrub native to West Africa. Ibogaine is a single, active alkaloid that is extracted from the iboga plant and provides a shorter journey than the plant itself. It has been traditionally used in spiritual ceremonies in African cultures, but in recent years, Ibogaine has gained attention for its potential in treating addiction, particularly opioid addiction.

Ibogaine therapy is more focused on medical or therapeutic outcomes, particularly in treating addiction, and does not involve the broader spiritual or ritualistic elements of an Iboga ceremony. Typically a session with Ibogaine lasts eight to 12 hours, whereas a traditional Iboga ceremony can last 24 to 36 hours. Both provide a deep introspective and visionary experience that often helps one reflect on the good and bad aspects of their life. Thus a heroin addict may be smacked with an awareness of how they've strayed off a healthy path and their life's purpose.

Ibogaine is known to affect multiple neurotransmitter systems simultaneously and is particularly noted for its effects on the brain's opioid receptors. It's believed to reset these receptors and alleviate withdrawal symptoms and cravings for opioids and other substances.

Some studies and anecdotal reports suggest that Ibogaine can significantly reduce withdrawal symptoms and cravings, potentially offering a rapid detoxification process for opioid addicts. Some users report a reduction in the desire for the addictive substance after Ibogaine treatment.

A study conducted in Mexico examined the effectiveness of Ibogaine and 5-MeO-DMT assisted therapy for trauma-exposed male Special Operations Forces Veterans. This study, affiliated with The Ohio State University and Johns Hopkins University, aims to understand the impact of these treatments on cognitive and mental health problems.[41,42,43]

Ibogaine itself is currently believed to have at least a 30% efficacy in treating opioid addiction, which is 10% better than what's achieved on average at drug rehabilitation centers. I feel a much higher success rate will be achieved with Ibogaine as they determine the number of sessions and potential synergies with DMT, integration, therapy, and other psychedelics as this research continues.

Ibogaine treatment can be risky. It has been associated with serious heart problems and can be fatal, particularly in individuals with pre-existing heart conditions. Arrhythmias, QT prolongation, Hypertension, Hypotension, chest pain, and rarely cardiac arrest may occur. Due to these risks, Ibogaine is not yet approved for medical use in many countries, including the United States, but in states like Colorado, personal possession of Ibogaine is now allowed.

For those planning to do Ibogaine therapy, I recommend a center that has continuous heart monitoring and a cardiologist on-site, should you have an arrhythmia. Of course, one should be thoroughly screened for heart disease prior to doing this therapy as well. I am hopeful that more progressive states, like Colorado, will soon be allowed to open safe Ibogaine treatment centers with fully integrated rehabilitation services and ongoing outpatient follow-up and support. This has the potential to save thousands of lives and millions of dollars, just by doing the simple math.

Psilocybin and LSD are being researched for the treatment of alcoholism. MDMA is being researched for substance abuse disorders, in addition to its known efficacy for PTSD, and Ayahuasca is also being looked at for potential benefits in treating addiction disorders. There is so much promise for the treatment of addiction disorders with psychedelics. We need to fund and accelerate psychedelic addiction research and invest in future centers as soon as possible.

Regulatory Developments

Decriminalization and future legislation towards legalization of various plant medicines and molecules show promise, but I remain concerned about over-regulation, high costs of permits/certifications, administrative burdens, medicalization, greed/control dynamics and so on, that could impede current progress. For example, the United States has fallen far behind Europe and Asia in regards to accessing emerging stem cell therapies due to an over-regulated and lobbyist-dominated/influenced medical system that has interestingly blocked access to many regenerative therapies that can make you well. Getting stem cell therapy for your knee may help prevent you from needing an expensive knee replacement or ongoing anti-inflammatory Rx's. Those who are lucky enough to have the resources can pay out of pocket or travel out of our country to receive more robust forms of this therapy, while the rest of us have more limited options that are reactive rather than proactive therapies.

Our system, unfortunately, thrives on keeping you sick and on as many pharmaceuticals as possible.

Improved accessibility and affordability to plant medicine is needed to treat the growing numbers of people who have depression, anxiety, and PTSD in our broken world, and our country that witnesses a mass shooting almost every day. This ongoing access must be maintained in the non-clinical world for it to be accessible to the broader community. Medicalization will continue to accelerate as investors pour more money into the growing for-profit psychedelic pharmaceutical industry.

Ethically and altruistically, it should not block the organic grass-roots evolution of natural medicine and shamanic healing communities offering plant medicine ceremonies. On the flip side, these natural healing communities must also learn to collaborate better and seek the greatest good for society, too. I've seen many in the community greedily charge as much as $3,000 for a single guided psilocybin journey with two integrations as they reply "namaste" after getting their Venmo. This nauseates me and is out of alignment with the field of plant medicine.

In addition to offering better affordability, and maintaining a safe set and settings, they should participate in committees in a non-isolationist stance to protect the plant medicine movement in the community at large.

Seeking collaboration with the regulatory and medical communities will help avoid pushback from them. I'm not saying they need to kiss ass. I'm implying that they need to be at the table in an intelligent and articulate way that expresses the core and essential need for this natural realm to thrive as well. The shamanic setting will provide greater opportunities for spiritual growth and awakening than what most medical clinics could offer.

Over the last few years, I've witnessed so many charlatans in the plant medicine community who consider themselves experts after a year and are unwilling to collaborate as a result of their inflated "know it all" and "I learned it all on YouTube" egos. I kindly encourage these folks to evolve themselves more spiritually and to be more cognizant of the depth and complexities of psychedelic work while embracing a humble state of being. Showing up to shout and rant unexpectedly at a conference podium will make them and our community look like idiots. We must all keep our egos in check, be life-long learners, and seek to understand and respect each other without hostility, seeking a common ground.

Pharmaceutical Developments

Is Big Pharma also seeking to repress emerging natural psychedelic therapies such as the evolving field of microdosing psilocybin?

Yes, I'm concerned that many of them may dispense lobbyist money to slow or block this movement, throwing pocket change from their typical annual budget of $300 million to protect their current and future assets! I continue to witness this happening as they attack small compounding pharmacies that minimally compete in the hormone replacement market.

It would be nice to legislate transparency to the public in terms of where their dollars go, but so much is hidden under the umbrellas of other groups. It's just a matter of time before they channel money through an elusive group named something like: "Americans for Safe Psychedelics," etc. The natural psychedelic grassroots movement will be a competitive threat to their up-and-coming expensive synthetic Rx analogs that will cost hundreds of dollars every month.

As usual, Pharma will create new FDA-approved analogs or delivery systems that will be cost-prohibitive, and unlikely to be covered by insurance. This is not a conspiracy, but simply an observation of the ongoing, non-altruistic, capitalistic, opportunistic, entrepreneurial spirit that our country idolizes. They will charge as much as the market and more wealthy consumers can tolerate, not what is reasonable and fair, thus making it financially inaccessible for most.

Concurrently, corporations will gain greater control of profits and tax deductions as politicians take their seemingly unlimited flow of lobbyist dollars to support new bills aimed at protecting their assets. Meanwhile, on Capitol Hill, a staff person reads your email to your Senator asking for the legalization of a plant medicine, drafts a vague, pasted response, and later schedules dinner with your Senator and the Pfizer lobbyist at a five-star restaurant to discuss new legislation aimed at blocking your access to plant medicine.

The threat to pharma's profit margins is real as the benefits from the Microdose.me study and simple word of mouth are leading many who suffer from depression to dump their Prozac to grow and capsulize the more therapeutic and cost-effective option of homegrown psilocybin mushrooms. The microdose.me study is a large-scale observational study conducted by a clinical psychology research team at the University of British Columbia, along with international researchers and partners. It involves thousands of participants from 84 countries, assessing the impact of microdosing psilocybin. Using a simple mobile phone app, it collects baseline and one-month follow-up data on participants' questionnaires and neurocognitive tasks. Preliminary findings suggest improvements in mood, depression, anxiety, and stress among microdosers compared to non-microdosers.[44]

Biotech companies leading the market share and currently wanting to replace your home microdosing regimen or SSRI include Mindset Pharma, Pfizer, Numinus Wellness, AbbVie, TRYP Therapeutics, Jazz Pharmaceuticals, MindMed, Filament Health Corp, Seelos Therapeutics, Inc., HAVN Life Sciences Inc., and COMPASS Pathways. Many more are emerging as investors realize the earning potentials. The gates of the corporate psychedelic derby have opened and we will have to wait to see who races ahead and wins by a nose to wear the roses.

In terms of research, COMPASS Pathways in the UK appears to have made the most notable clinical advances in psilocybin-based treatments for mental health conditions, and recently published results for investigational COMP360 (synthetic psilocybin) for efficacy in treatment-resistant bipolar type II disorder (bipolar II).[45]

They are also researching the impacts of their synthetic psilocybin in treatment-resistant depression, PTSD, and anorexia nervosa.

The advantages of synthetic oral versions of psilocybin may include better efficacy, fewer side effects, improved bioavailability and absorption, and precise dosing for the treatment of depression and other conditions. This will be ideal for many with this pharmacological purity who are not interested in growing or preparing psilocybin for journey work or microdosing. For those of us who enjoy the hobby, we can achieve many of these goals by sourcing high-quality spores, and using the Lemon-Tek technique to purify the dried mushrooms in our kitchens.

A couple of years ago I attended a four day live portion of an MAPS MDMA course to learn how to safely use this molecule for the treatment of PTSD. This followed some initial virtual sessions. Unfortunately the FDA rejected MDMA for use in PTSD in August 2024. As a result myself and others will be unable to offer this to so many who need this effective therapy, and as a result more suicides will sadly occur. The conference was held at the recently constructed Usona Institute on the outskirts of Madison, Wisconsin. Co-founded in 2014 by Bill Linton, CEO and Founder of the international life sciences company Promega Corporation, and Malynn Utzinger, MD, Director of Integrative Practices at Promega Corporation. This facility is a state-of-the-art creation that incorporates meeting spaces and meditation rooms perfectly designed to facilitate the R&D of psychedelic medicines. The space is being made available for non-profits and other groups who are learning about psychedelic medicine or are involved in research. Seeing and experiencing the energy of this space created by Bill and Malynn and the team was beyond my imagination, and I was impressed with their meticulous attention to aesthetic detail noted in the architectural, interior, and flowing landscape design.

Most importantly, the Usona Institute shows how large biotech corporations can give back to the community of psychedelic medicine by manifesting this space and the beautifully landscaped grounds around it to foster advances in the field. The unique meditation spaces include rooms such as a holographic light and sound room, a water experience room, a sound healing room, a tropical room, and a Harry Potter-like room. I'm hopeful that someday I can hold a retreat and experience each room with legalized plant medicines! Catching Bill between talks over dinner, he informed me how Promega and the Usona Institute have two ongoing studies: one on injectable 5-MeO-DMT and the other on Psilocybin.[46]

With continued research and clinical validation, we remain hopeful that both MDMA and DMT will eventually gain regulatory approval. Even in the most optimistic scenario, this process will likely take several more years—but the momentum is building. I'm especially excited about the potential of the long-acting intramuscular DMT.

In addition to creating new molecular structures of plant medicines and analogs of existing synthetics, ongoing research is also exploring optimal delivery methods.

New delivery psychedelic methods include:

- Transdermal patches.

- Implantable slow-release devices.

- Liposomal formulations.

- Sublingual/buccal formulations.

- Nasal sprays (a similar concept as the FDA-approved Spravato, a nasal esketamine spray).

- Inhalation devices, such as vapes.

- Injectable forms, such as an intramuscular sustained release DMT. Of course, some of these deliveries already exist from underground sources, too, but hopefully we'll see FDA-approved versions in the next decade.

In summary, I am not opposed to pharmaceutical companies researching and developing more effective analogs of psychedelics or delivery modalities. I am also forever grateful for the hundreds of life-saving medications including antibiotics, antivirals, vaccines, cardiovascular and anti-cancer medications that have been developed to date. I am simply calling out the ongoing greedy behavior of the corporate pharmaceutical companies in regards to opportunistic price gouging of old existing medications like Epipens or Insulin, as well as the extremely high costs of new medications, especially immunologics. I'm hopeful they will ethically trend themselves towards greater affordability, and that politicians will seek to bring down the costs of all medications which on average are 400% more in the United States for the same medications compared to prices in other countries. I also feel that the tireless, genius biotech researchers are often the unsung heroes of society and should be recognized more, rather than movie stars, rockstars, and professional athletes, in my opinion.

I'd like to see business leaders transform themselves and their companies into conscious, responsible businesses looking out for the greater good, rather than impressing their friends with an invite on their private jets to their beachside villa on Grand Cayman. Flying into Burning Man on their private jets and broadcasting themselves as spiritual, hip, and environmentally conscious doesn't hold water, either. As mentioned, the Usona Institute is an example of conscious leadership, contributing altruistically towards the advancement of psychedelic medicine.

Many pharmaceutical corporate homepages profess to be making their products available in an all-inclusive and accessible to all manner. Do they mean a one-month discount GoodRx coupon or long-term affordability? That's a joke. I challenge all of them to follow through with the authenticity of these claims and I'll applaud their actions in my next book if they prove and succeed in doing so. From corporate leaders to therapists, facilitators, physicians and shamans, we must all lead and heal from our hearts. By doing so, we will still find financial stability, affordability for the masses, and most importantly an opportunity to change the world by helping all of us shift our consciousness to lead a happier, more loving life of giving.

Chapter 14

Supportive Therapies to Optimize Your Psychedelic Sacred Sexuality Experiences

As a Functional Medicine physician, I've always been passionate about nutrition, mitochondrial optimization, hormone balancing, heart health, brain health, gut health, and finding/treating the root causes of inflammation, to name a few. Of course, a healthy lifestyle and mindfulness hold equal importance as well.

I strongly feel that we can enhance our psychedelic experience by looking at systems more holistically. By doing so, we can optimize the regenerative and neuroplastic benefits often offered by psychedelics to potentially make us happier, smarter, and more creative. The field of biohacking, deployed by many DIY (do it yourself) wellness enthusiasts like Dave Asprey, Ben Greenfield, and others, often explores the benefits of nootropics and other modalities on brain health, but in my observations frequently misses a few important check marks on the list. It's both an art and science that requires more extensive testing to find abnormalities in methylation pathways, dysbiosis (gut imbalances), hormone balancing of sex/thyroid/adrenal/growth hormone axis, mitochondrial function, and so much more. While you don't have to go crazy exploring these realms extensively, it's important to at least have a functional or integrative medicine provider throw a medium-sized net and check these things.

Let's start with nutrition. I'm not going to go down the rabbit hole of discussing Paleo, Keto, or Mediterranean diets, as that's the subject of a few books. I'd simply encourage you to maintain a healthy balanced organic diet that helps you maintain a normal BMI and is personalized for you by a nutritionist to help address things such as inflammation, food allergies, or means to lower your glucose and or cholesterol. I eat a basic Mediterranean diet, free of red meat, and rarely drink alcohol. It's rich in omega-3s, fiber, and nutrients from veggies. I do keep the carbs to a minimum, though.

Supplementing with the following should be considered:

- A high-quality multivitamin that contains methyl folate and methyl B12 in addition to other B vitamins and minerals.

- Vitamin D3 with K2 at a more robust dose of 5,000 IU of D is important for your brain, immune system, and bone health.

- Omega-3 balanced formula of DHA and EPA, two to four grams daily.

- NAD+, Nicotinamide Adenine Dinucleotide, is a vital coenzyme for mitochondrial health. In my opinion, it may be the most important supplement of them all. It can be supplemented by taking a precursor NMN (Nicotinamide Mononucleotide) in the range of 250 mg to 1000 mg/day. (Liposomal forms are best.) The older you are, the more you'll need. IV or Sub-Q doses of NAD+ are the most effective in elevating levels, which can then be maintained with NMN orally. Additional IV or SubQ can be added periodically to further optimize, as tailored by your physician. Soon I hope we can check levels and adjust more accurately. My personal favorite route is NAD+ SubQ 100mg twice weekly with daily NMN.

- Methylene Blue, at a dose of 25mg daily (capsule or liquid), has been a game-changer for many of my patients—boosting energy, sharpening cognition, and uplifting mood through its profound mitochondrial-enhancing effects. By optimizing the electron transport chain and increasing ATP production, it supports cellular vitality while offering potent neuroprotection. Interestingly, Methylene Blue can also heighten sensitivity to psychedelics, amplifying their effects. For this reason, I recommend pausing it for a couple of days before any psychedelic journey to ensure a smooth and balanced experience.

- Glutathione, 500 to 1000 mg a day reduces oxidative stress on the brain and body, helps with detoxing, is anti-inflammatory, supports mitochondrial support, neurotransmitter balance, and cellular repair, to name a few. An IV push of glutathione can help one more rapidly recover from fatigue related to MDMA journeys in combination with the usual stack of NAC, 5-HTP, Grape Seed Extract, etc.

- Co-Q10, 100 mg/day. Also reduces oxidative stress, supports mitochondrial function, and is neuroprotective. Individuals on statins should all be taking Coq10.

- Resveratrol, 250mg/day is an antioxidant found in red grapes that may help protect against neurodegenerative disease and promote lengthening of your telomeres.

- Curcumin supplement or dietary sources. 500-1000mg by supplement can help reduce brain and systemic inflammation.

- Daily balanced probiotic.

- Other brain health supplements to consider include: Acetyl L-Carnitine, Phosphatidylserine, L-Theanine, and Gingko. Of course, there are many more I could mention, but again, this would take up an entire book.

If you want to keep things simple, stick with a multivitamin, Vitamin D, and Omega-3. You can add others on the list if you'd like to take things another notch higher down the road. Of course, you can get many of these things in your diet as well and ignore the list if desired.

Hormone Balancing

Hormones have a profound effect on one's neurotransmitter balance. As you get older, especially over 50, it's a good idea to have your levels checked, typically by blood, and balancing them if desired, and without contraindications such as history of blood clots, breast cancer, or prostate cancer. Any woman with a first-degree family history of breast cancer (i.e.: mother or sister) needs to avoid or do low-hormone replacement with close physician monitoring, annual breast cancer screening, and caution. Bioidentical hormones are best, meaning they are of the same structure your body produces.

Neurohormonal impacts (how various hormones impact neurotransmitters).

- Testosterone promotes healthy dopamine levels (passion, sex drive). To improve libido, I've found it best to optimize testosterone levels in men and women first before reaching for the peptide PT-141.

- Estrogen promotes healthy serotonin levels (happy, relaxed).

- Progesterone promotes healthy Gaba levels (relaxation, sleep).

Balancing hormones may reduce your risk of Alzheimer's. A recent 2023 study published in the European Journal of Endocrinology found that more optimal testosterone and IGF-1 (growth hormone) levels may reduce one's risk of developing Alzheimer's disease.[47]

What is the best way to balance hormones? Under the guidance of a provider with expertise in hormones, one can balance hormones best using topical creams or hormone pellets. Oral progesterone can be taken for women at night, but oral estrogens and testosterone should be avoided due to the increased risks of blood clots. For gals, I recommend hormone pellet therapy or topical bioidentical creams.

For guys, pellets are great, except in some who have minimal body fat. The next best option is one or two times a week injectable testosterone or a testosterone gel/cream. Estrogen metabolites need to be monitored and managed in men undergoing testosterone therapy.

Women need annual breast and uterine cancer screening, and men need annual prostate cancer screening. Over the last 20 years, I've noticed more men in their thirties with testosterone deficiency, which may be related to environmental toxins, stress, lack of exercise, and other factors yet to be determined. This trend is worrisome. Some women seem to be experiencing early menopause as well.

Balancing Your Microbiome

The GI system produces the majority of serotonin, and an imbalanced microbiome can contribute to a neurotransmitter imbalance as well. If you struggle with irregular bowel patterns, bloating, cramping, etc., I strongly encourage you to have your microbiome tested by a functional medicine physician or gastroenterologist. Doing so can help identify pathogens, overgrowths of bacteria, or deficiencies of good bacteria that may be creating inflammation. This can be treated with things like probiotics, prebiotics, digestive enzymes, antibiotics, and dietary modifications based on findings. Sometimes all 'ya need is a probiotic. Doing so can often help overweight individuals lose some pounds, too!

Detoxing

This can often be maintained simply by eating a clean organic diet, and doing a robust once-a-week Glutathione, Vitamin C, and Calcium D-Glucarate cocktail before a workout or sauna session. It's reasonable to test for heavy metals and other toxins with your provider, especially if you're a sushi eater, or live in Flint, Michigan. If high levels are noted, you may be a candidate for IV EDTA to more aggressively clear these out.

Detox Supplement Dose Recommendations:

- Liposomal Glutathione 1000 mg

- Vitamin C 1000 mg

- Calcium D-Glucarate 1000 mg

Peptide Therapy

Peptides are a rapidly emerging area of medicine showing immense promise towards reducing inflammation, tissue regeneration, assisting with weight loss and libido, and optimizing growth hormone levels. The most common peptides that most everyone knows are GLP-1 peptides (Glucagon-Like Peptide-1) such as Ozembic (Semaglutide) and Mounjaro (tirzepatide) prescribed for Type 2 diabetes and/or weight loss. These weight loss peptides have been so effective that grocery stores worry about lost revenue in food purchases, meanwhile, airlines are happy to note less jet fuel consumption with lighter passenger loads!!

These weight loss peptides are FDA-approved, along with other GLP-1, but others such as Ipamorelin and CJC-1295, which act to stimulate our own growth hormone production, are being taken off the market by the FDA. These peptides work by mimicking GHRH (growth hormone-releasing hormone) which then helps stimulate the release of your own growth hormone levels. These have been available for off-label use prescribed by regenerative medicine doctors, but now have been removed from the market for unclear reasons. Is the FDA truly waiting for additional research to show safety and efficacy? Or is Pharma lobbying to block access to this class of regenerative peptides as they feel a potential loss from people getting well? This is the multibillion dollar question.

Currently, there are 60 peptide-based therapeutics in the market and more than 500 in the development stages. I'm hopeful that our regulatory system will be more supportive of regenerative therapies, rather than sick-medicine therapies, and approve these shortly. Artificial intelligence should be able to accelerate the evaluation of the safety and efficacy of emerging therapies in the future. However, the bureaucracy of the FDA, lobbyists, and politics will continue to slow this process.

For those of you who may be taking a weight loss peptide, be sure to hold it the week before and the week of an Ayahuasca, Peyote, as it could increase the potential for nausea during plant medicine ceremonies. Of course, it's always a good idea to discuss this with your provider, too.

Why mention all of these things? Because in doing so, you'll optimize your sexual health and your overall wellness! Most significantly, keeping your hormones balanced as you head into your fifties and beyond can help you enjoy sex for more decades and improve your healthspan and quality of life. My goal is not to simply inform you how to go deeper with your lover while enjoying psychedelics, but to help you maintain your youthful mojo for decades to come!

Chapter 15

Final Thoughts

In summary, I'd like to again thank you for your boldness and curiosity that motivated you to pick up this book!

My goal has been to share the insights and knowledge I've gained over the past 20-plus years to help you and others find a deeper meaning in your life. Yes, we can find meaning through religious and philosophical pursuits, but the deepest meaning is that which you discover within yourself. You don't need a guru if you have the strength and willingness to go within.

If you have suggestions for improving this second edition, I would truly appreciate your feedback through the Psychedelic SacredSexuality.com contact me page. I will personally review them and do my best to improve future editions.

Psychedelics can provide the catalyst to soften your over-thinking default mode network allowing you to see, feel, and experience your deeper essence, your light body, and your expansive connections to the world and universe around you. As you do so, you will learn to share this field with your lover, and can further expand this field into the realms of oneness and ecstasy.

Energetically, this book is nothing more than a gift from my heart to yours, to help you find, explore, and manifest this pure unconditional love for yourself, your lover, and the world. I want nothing more than for beings to experience these higher realms of love during our short existence on this planet. Wishing you the best in your life's journey, and may your presence help make our planet a more peaceful, joyful, and sustainable place to enjoy.

About the Author

Astraeus Amori is an Integrative and Functional Medicine healer, whose 30-plus years of clinical practice and expertise spans diverse healing modalities. With a deep reverence for the interconnectedness of mind, body, and spirit, he seamlessly integrates shamanism, natural plant-based therapies, energy medicine, and sound healing into his practice. By harmoniously blending these ancient wisdom traditions with modern medical approaches, Astraeus offers a holistic and transformative healing experience.

Beyond his diverse healing abilities, Astraeus Amori is a dedicated planetary grid worker. Recognizing the inherent power of quartz crystals, he has intuitively placed hundreds of these in strategic locations across the globe. Through this intentional act, he endeavors to reestablish the long-forgotten connections between ancient energies, fostering a harmonious balance within Gaia during these challenging times.

In his quest for wisdom and enlightenment, Astraeus Amori delves into deep meditation, embarks on profound personal plant medicine journeys, and draws inspiration from the celestial bodies above. His writings, enriched by these spiritual practices, emanate a profound wisdom that resonates with individuals vibrating at a similar open-heart frequency of love and oneness.

Guided by his intention to awaken beings on Earth, he illuminates the path to profound self-love and compassion for all sentient beings.

Nestled amidst the soulful mountain landscapes of Colorado, Astraeus Amori calls this enchanting place home. However, he frequently embarks on transformative journeys to regions of shamanic significance, seeking insights and participating in plant medicine retreats. These sacred voyages allow him to deepen his understanding of Indigenous wisdom and expand his healing repertoire.

Astraeus Amori stands as a radiant beacon of light in the realm of healing, inspiring and guiding countless individuals towards personal transformation, inner healing, and universal love.

About Autumn Skye

Artist of the "Beloved" painting on cover

Autumn Skye lives, breathes, and dreams art, and has done so since she was old enough to hold a pencil and reach for a piece of paper. Her childhood and early adult years were spent traveling the landscapes of both her wild Canadian backyard and distant international shores. Through her wanderlust, she developed a deep reverence for the beauty of nature and the diversity of humanity and continuously endeavors to translate this inspiration through her work.

As a self-taught artist, she is forever a student of the intuitively creative process. Autumn Skye's style weaves together refined realism, iconic imagery, archetypal symbolism, and spiritual principles. She's inspired by the magnificence of this incredible planet, the potency of these extraordinary times, and the mysteries of the cosmos. Through her work, she seeks to honor the resiliency of the human spirit and the intricate connections between all facets of life.

Autumn Skye exhibits and teaches worldwide, and otherwise thrives and paints in the beautiful temperate rainforest of coastal British Columbia, Canada. Considering herself immensely blessed to do what feeds her soul, she strives to support others through creative empowerment, the gift of beauty, and the perpetuation of inspiration. Source: https://autumnskyeart.com/about

References

1. Michael Pollan, *How to Change Your Mind: What the New Science of Psychedelics Teaches Us About Consciousness, Dying, Addiction, Depression, and Transcendence* (New York: Penguin Press, 2018); *How to Change Your Mind,* directed by Lucy Walker and Alison Ellwood (Jigsaw Productions, 2022), Docuseries.

2. Paul Stamnts, *Fantastic Fungi: How Mushrooms Can Heal, Shift Consciousness, and Save the Planet* (Earth Aware Editions, 2019).

3. "Proposition 122: Access to Natural Psychedelic Substances." Legislative Council Draft. (Colorado), https://leg.colorado.gov/sites/default/files/initiative%2520referendum_proposition%20122%20final%20lc%20packet.pdf.

4. Hannes Kettner, Sam Gandy, Eline C. H. M. Haijen, and Robin L. Carhart-Harris. 2019. "From Egoism to Ecoism: Psychedelics Increase Nature Relatedness in a State-Mediated and Context-Dependent Manner," *International Journal of Environmental Research and Public Health* 16, no. 24 (December 2019): 5147, https://doi.org/10.3390/ijerph16245147.

5. Alicia Rohan, "Study suggests psychedelic drugs could reduce criminal behavior," *The University of Alabama News,* October 17, 2017, https://www.uab.edu/news/research/item/8802-study-suggests-psychedelic-drugs-could-reduce-criminal-behavior.

6. Wickliffe C, Abraham, "Metaplasticity: tuning synapses and networks for plasticity," *Nature Reviews Neuroscience* 9, no. 387 (May 2008). https://doi.org/10.1038/nrn2356

7. Samantha Morse and Greg Ferenstein, "The Lab: Is Microdosing Bad for your Heart?" *Third Wave,* https://thethirdwave.co/research/microdosing-bad-for-your-heart/.

8.   Anahita Anais, "Everything You Need to Know About Choosing A Microdosing Protocol," *Microdose Guru,* December 27, 2021, https://www.microdoseguru.com/post/everything-you-need-to-know-about-choosing-a-microdosing-protocol.

9.   "A Multi-Site Phase 3 Study of MDMA-Assisted Therapy for PTSD (MAPP1)," Multidisciplinary Association for Psychedelic Studies, https://maps.org/mdma/ptsd/mapp1/.

10.   Dr. Dave Rabin, MD, PhD, "Can MDMA-Assisted Therapy Repair our Epigenetics with Dr. Candace Lewis PhD," *The Psychedelic Report,* podcast audio, October 17, 2023, https://www.thepsychedelic.report/can-mdma-assisted-therapy-repair-our-epigenetics-with-dr-candace-lewis-phd/.

11.   Rafael Moliner, et al. "Psychedelics promote plasticity by directly binding to BDNF receptor TrkB," *Nature Neuroscience* 26 (June 2023): 1032–1041. https://doi.org/10.1038/s41593-023-01316-5.

12.   Hannes Kettner, Sam Gandy, Eline C. H. M. Haijen, and Robin L. Carhart-Harris. 2019. "From Egoism to Ecoism: Psychedelics Increase Nature Relatedness in a State-Mediated and Context-Dependent Manner," *International Journal of Environmental Research and Public Health* 16, no. 24 (December 2019): 5147, https://doi.org/10.3390/ijerph16245147.

13.   Matthias Forstmann and Christina Sagioglou, "Lifetime experience with (classic) psychedelics predicts pro-environmental behavior through an increase in nature relatedness," *Journal of Psychopharmacology* 31, no. 8 (June 2017): 975-988, https://doi.org/10.1177/0269881117714049.

14.   Christina Sagioglou and Matthias Forstmann, "Psychedelic use predicts objective knowledge about climate change via increases in nature relatedness," *Drug Science, Policy and Law* 8 (October 2022), https://doi.org/10.1177/20503245221129803.

15.   Mattias Forstmann, et al., "Among psychedelic-experienced users, only past use of psilocybin reliably predicts nature relatedness," *Journal of Psychopharmacology* 37, no. 1 (January 2023): 93-106, https://doi.org/10.1177/02698811221146356.

16. Kurn von Hungen, Sidney Roberts, and Diane F. Hill, "LSD as an agonist and antagonist at central dopamine receptors," *Nature* 252 (December 1974): 588–589, https://doi.org/10.1038/252588a0.

17. V. J. Watts, et al., "LSD and structural analogs: Pharmacological evaluation at D_1 dopamine receptors," *Psychopharmacology* 118 (April 1995): 401–409, https://doi.org/10.1007/BF02245940.

18. Torsten Passie, et al., "The pharmacology of Lysergic Acid Diethylamide: A Review," *CNS Neuroscience and Therapeutics* 14, no. 4 (November 2008):295-314, https://doi.org/10.1111/j.1755-5949.2008.00059.x.

19. Mattias E. Liechti, "Modern Clinical Research on LSD," *Neuropsychopharmacology* 42, no. 11 (April 2017): 2114-2127, https://doi.org/10.1038/npp.2017.86.

20. Daniel I. Brierley and Colin Davidson, "Developments in harmine pharmacology – Implications for ayahuasca use and drug-dependence treatment," *Progress in Neuro-Psychopharmacology and Biological Psychiatry* 39, no. 2 (December 2012): 263-272, https://doi.org/10.1016/j.pnpbp.2012.06.001.

21. David Wolinsky, Frederick Streeter Barrett, and Ryan Vandrey, "The psychedelic effects of cannabis: A review of the literature," *Journal of Psychopharmacology* (November 2023), https://doi.org/10.1177/02698811231209194.

22. Ethan B. Russo, "Taming THC: potential cannabis synergy and phytocannabinoid-terpenoid entourage effects," *British Journal of Pharmacology* 163, no. 7 (July 2011): 1344-64, https://doi.org/10.1111/j.1476-5381.2011.01238.x.

23. Daniel McQueen, *Psychedelic Cannabis: Therapeutic Methods and Unique Blends to Treat Trauma and Transform Consciousness* (Vermont: Park Street Press, 2021).

24. Nicole Napoli, "Frequent Marijuana Use Linked to Heart Disease," *American College of Cardiology,* February 24, 2023, https://www.acc.org/About-ACC/Press-Releases/2023/02/23/18/53/Frequent-Marijuana-Use-Linked-to-Heart-Disease.

25. Robert Simmons and Naisha Ahsain, *The Book of Stones: Who They Are and What They Teach,* (Vermont: Destiny Books, 2015).

26.   "The Health Effects of Cannabis and Cannabinoids: The Current State of Evidence and Recommendations for Research," *National Academies of Sciences, Engineering, and Medicine,* January 12, 2017, https://www.ncbi.nlm.nih.gov/books/NBK425767/.

27.   "The Health Effects of Cannabis and Cannabinoids: The Current State of Evidence and Recommendations for Research," *National Academies of Sciences, Engineering, and Medicine,* January 12, 2017, https://www.ncbi.nlm.nih.gov/books/NBK425767/.

28.   Tony Antoniou, PhD, Jack Bodkin, and Joanne M. W. Ho, "Drug interactions with cannabinoids," *Canadian Medical Association Journal* 192, no. 9 (March 2020): E206, https://doi.org/10.1503%2Fcmaj.191097.

29.   Anees Bahji, Gustavo H. Vazquez, Carlos A. Zarate, Jr., "Comparative efficacy of racemic ketamine and esketamine for depression: A systematic review and meta-analysis," *J Affect Disord* 278 (January 2021): 542-555, https://doi.org/10.1016/j.jad.2020.09.071.

30.   Jeremy Narby, *Cosmic Serpent: DNA and the Origins of Knowledge,* (Jeremy P. Tarcher/Putnam, 1999).

31.   Michael Harner, *The Way of the Shaman,* (California: HarperOne, 1990).

32.   Daniel I. Brierley and Colin Davidson, "Developments in harmine pharmacology – Implications for ayahuasca use and drug-dependence treatment," *Progress in Neuro-Psychopharmacology and Biological Psychiatry* 39, no. 2 (December 2012): 263-272, https://doi.org/10.1016/j.pnpbp.2012.06.001.

33.   Theresa M. Carbonaro and Michael B. Gatch, "Neuropharmacology of N,N-dimethyltryptamine," *Brain Research Bulletin* 126, no. 1 (September 2016): 74-88, https://doi.org/10.1016/j.brainresbull.2016.04.016.

34.   Rafael Guimarães dos Santos, PhD, "Immunological Effects of Ayahuasca in Humans," *Journal of Psychoactive Drugs* 46 (November 2014): 383-8, https://doi.org/10.1080/02791072.2014.960113.

35.   Attila Szabo, et al., "Psychedelic N,N-dimethyltryptamine and 5-methoxy-N,N-dimethyltryptamine modulate innate and adaptive inflammatory responses through the sigma-1 receptor of human monocyte-

derived dendritic cells," *PLoS One* 9, no. 8 (August 2014): E106533, https://doi.org/10.1371/journal.pone.0106533.

36.   Harmine, Harmaline, and Tetrahydroharmine. Reversible inhibition of monoamine oxidase-A or 'RIMA' type MAOIs that temporarily limit metabolism of monoamine neurotransmitters or other tryptamines such as serotonin and DMT. Harmala alkaloids may have additional pharmacology that contributes to the mechanisms of Ayahuasca including: Binding of dual specificity tyrosine phosphorylated and regulated kinase 1A (DYRK1A), 5HT2A/2C receptors, Imidazoline I2 receptors, and the Dopamine Transporter (DAT)

37.   Alissa Hirshfield-Flores, "DMT: The Spirit Molecule: A Doctor's Revolutionary Research into the Biology of Near-Death and Mystical Experiences," *The American Journal of Psychiatry* 159, no. 8 (August 2002): 1261-1455, https://doi.org/10.1176/appi.ajp.159.8.1448.

38.   J Ott, "Pharmahuasca: human pharmacology of oral DMT plus harmine," *J Psychoactive Drugs* 31, no. 2 (April-June 1999): 171-7, https://doi.org/10.1080/02791072.1999.10471741.

39.   Shelby Hartman, "Rick Strassman on DMT and the Mystical State," *Double Blind Magazine,* March 12, 2021, https://doubleblindmag.com/rick-strassman-dmt-mystical-state/.

40.   Alan K. Davis, et al., "Survey of entity encounter experiences occasioned by inhaled N,N-dimethyltryptamine: Phenomenology, interpretation, and enduring effects," *J Psychopharmacology* 34, no. 9 (April 2020): 1008-1020, https://doi.org/10.1177/0269881120916143.

41.   Alan Kooi Davis, et al. "Open-label study of consecutive ibogaine and 5-MeO-DMT assisted-therapy for trauma-exposed male Special Operations Forces Veterans: prospective data from a clinical program in Mexico," *The American Journal of Drug and Alcohol Abuse* 46, no. 5 (November 2023): 587-596, https://doi.org/10.1080/00952990.2023.2220874.

42.   Emily Caldwell, "Psychedelics improve mental health, cognition in special ops veterans," *Ohio State News,* October 5, 2023, https://news.osu.edu/psychedelics-improve-mental-health-cognition-in-special-ops-veterans/.

43. Katie Snow, "New Psychedelic Drug Ibogaine offers new hope in the addiction battle," *Today* video, December 12, 2023, https://www.today.com/video/new-psychedelic-drug-ibogaine-offers-new-hope-in-addiction-battle-200114245581?search=ibogaine.

44. Joseph M. Rootman, et al., "Psilocybin microdosers demonstrate greater observed improvements in mood and mental health at one month relative to non-microdosing controls," *Scientific Reports* 12, no. 11091 (June 2022), https://doi.org/10.1038/s41598-022-14512-3.

45. Scott T. Aaronson, MD, et al., "Single-Dose Synthetic Psilocybin With Psychotherapy for Treatment-Resistant Bipolar Type II Major Depressive Episodes: A Nonrandomized Controlled Trial," *JAMA Psychiatry,* December 06, 2023, https://doi.org/10.1001/jamapsychiatry.2023.4685.

46. "5-MeO-DMT," Usona Institute, https://www.usonainstitute.org/5-meo-dmt.

47. Chris Ho Ching Yeung, et al., "The influence of growth and sex hormones on risk of Alzheimer's disease: a mendelian randomization study," *European Journal of Epidemiology* 38, no. 7 (July 2023): 745-755, https://doi.org/10.1007/s10654-023-01015-2.

Plant medicine Pharmacological Summaries by Spirit pharmacist Ben Malcolm PharmD.

References

Illustrations (please update with page numbers when ready in final book)

Tantric Art from Nepal. (iStock 485636339), page 4

Goddess Parvati. (DALL-E generated AI art by the author), page 15

Lord Shiva. (DALL-E generated AI art by the author), page 16

Lord Ardhanarishvara. (DALL-E generated AI art by the author), page 16

Yab-Yum (DALL-E generated AI art by the author), page 21

An Alchemy of Divine Masculine and Feminine Energies (DALL-E generated AI art by the author), page 32

Quartz Crystals applied to chakras for energy balancing. (Sketch by Ewa Kienko), page 34

Balancing the Third Chakra with Sacred Geometric Form. (DALL-E generated AI art by the author), page 35

Sacred Geometric Form (Photo by Author), page 36

Tantric Massage (Sketch by Ewa Kienko), page 37

Bedside treats (DALL-E generated AI art.), page 39

Women with mushrooms (DALL-E generated AI art by the author), page 43

Psilocybin Mushrooms (Shutterstock 507739813), page 45

Brain QEEG before and after psilocybin In "Science Graphic of the Week." Petri et al., page 46

Proceedings of the Royal society Interface, https://www.wired.com/2014/10/magic-mushrooms-brain/, page 46

Spinning crystal healing bowl on third chakra (Sketch by Ewa Kienko), page 51

Tantric Sound healing of root chakra with Tibetan bowl. (Sketch by Ewa Kienko), page 52

References

LSD structure (Shutterstock 221743492), page 139

THC and CBD structure (Shutterstock 221743399 and 222815482), page 159

Ketamine structure (iStock 506904156), page 175

Ayahuasca image (Shutterstock 1131880895), page 180

DMT structure (Shutterstock 223966174), page 203

Rapeh ceremony (Sketch by Ewa Kienko), page 209

Third eye connect (Sketch by Ewa Kienko), page 211

Honey Bee with Spiral Galaxy eye (Created in Dall-e January 2024 by the author), back cover

Resources

Recommended Reading

Pollan, Michael. *How To Change Your Mind: What the New Science of Psychedelics Teaches Us About Consciousness, Dying, Addition, Depression, and Transcendence.* Penguin Press, 2018.

Strassman, Rick. *DMT: The Spirit Molecule: A Doctor's Revolutionary Research into the Biology of Near-Death and Mystical Experiences.* Park Street Press, 2001.

Shulgin, Alexander T., and Ann Shulgin. *TIHKAL: The Continuation.* Transform Press, 1997.

Miller, Richard L. Psychedelic Medicine: *The Healing Powers of LSD, MDMA, Psilocybin, and Ayahuasca.* Park Street Press, 2017.

Kotler, Steven and Wheal, Jamie. *Stealing Fire: How Silicon Valley, the Navy Seals, and Maverick Scientists Are Revolutionizing the Way We Live and Work.* 2017

Nuwer, Rachel. *I Feel Love: MDMA and the Quest for Connection in a Fractured World* by

Stamets, Paul. *Mycelium Running: How Mushrooms Can Help Save the World.* Ten Speed Press, 2005.

Fadiman, James. *The Psychedelic Explorer's Guide: Safe, Therapeutic, and Sacred Journeys.* Park Street Press, 2011.

Mandrake, K., and Haze, Virginia. *The Psilocybin Mushroom Bible: The Definitive Guide to Growing and Using Magic Mushrooms.* Green Candy Press, 2016.

Tafur, Joseph. *The Fellowship of the River.* A medical doctor's exploration into Traditional Amazonian Plant Medicine. 2017

Funder, Christian. *Grandmother Ayahuasca: Plant Medicine and the Psychedelic Brain*. Park Street Press, 2021.

Hoag, Greg and Gail. Sacred Geometry, The Universal Language of Divine Alignment. 2024

Shaman, Healer. *Sage: How to Heal Yourself and Others with the Energy Medicine of the Americas* by Alberto Villoldo Ph.D. 2000

The Humming Effect: Sound Healing for Health and Happiness. By Jonathan and Andi Goldman. 2017

Beaulieu, John. *Human Tuning: Sound Healing With Tuning Forks*. 2010

Grover, Fred Jr. *Spiritual Genomics, A physician's deep dive beyond modern medicine, discovering unique keys to optimizing DNA health, longevity and happiness!* 2019

Simmons,Robert, Ahsian, Naisha. *The Book of Stones: Who They Are and What They Teach Us*. Destiny Books; third Edition, Revised Mar 10, 2015.

Williamson, Elysabeth. *The Pleasures and Principles of Partner Yoga*. 2004 https://partneryoga.net/

Check out the Maps bookshop for more great reads- https://maps.org/product-category/bookshop/

Psychedelic Podcasts to consider:

Psychedelic Podcast

Psychedelics Today Podcast

Luminous, A Series about Psychedelics by NPR

The Psychedelic Report with Dave Rabin

The Joe Rogan Experience

Huberman Lab

Psychedelic Research Centers

Multidisciplinary Association For Psychedelic Studies (MAPS) Research https://maps.org/about-maps/mission/

Johns Hopkins Center for Psychedelic and Consciousness Research https://hopkinspsychedelic.org/

John Hopkins Medicine Psychedelics Research and Psilocybin Therapy https://www.hopkinsmedicine.org/psychiatry/research/psychedelics-research

Stanford Psychedelic Science Group https://med.stanford.edu/spsg.html?tab=proxy

Library of Research on All Psychedelic Medicines https://psychedelicmedicineassociation.org/resources/

Imperial College London's Centre for Psychedelic Research

https://www.imperial.ac.uk/psychedelic-research-centre/

Usona Institute https://www.usonainstitute.org/

Training and Education in Psychedelics
Multidisciplinary Association of Psychedelic Studies

Maps.org

Naropa Center for Psychedelic Studies https://www.naropa.edu/academics/schools-centers/center-for-psychedelic-studies/

California Institute of Integral Studies (CIIS), Center for Psychedelic Therapies and Research https://www.ciis.edu/research-centers-and-initiatives/center-for-psychedelic-therapies-and-research

Compass Pathway Training and Research: https://compasspathways.com/our-work/therapist-training/

Prati Psychedelic Research and Training Institute Ketamine-Assisted Psychotherapy (KAP)

https://pratigroup.org/kap-training/

Psychedelics Today Courses: https://psychedelicstoday.com/online-courses/

Fluence Psychedelic Training https://www.fluencetraining.com/training/

Psychedelic Medicine Association Training: https://psychedelicmedicineassociation.org/webinars/

Chacruna Institute Training: https://chacruna.net/trainings/

Center for Medicinal Mindfulness https://medicinalmindfulness.org/training/

Non-Profit Psychedelic Organizations

Maps https://maps.org/about-maps/mission/

Zendo Project (https://zendoproject.org/resources/

Fireside Project https://firesideproject.org/

The Nowak Society, https://www.thenowaksociety.org/

Psychedelic clubs in the United States : https://www.psychedeliclub.com/

Psychedelic Association Europe: https://www.psychedelicseurope.org/

Psychedelic Society UK: https://psychedelicsociety.org.uk/

A short list of musicians who resonate well with psychedelic sacred sexuality!

Yaima, Porangui, Alex Cruz, Rufus du Sol, Desert Dwellers, Liquid Bloom, East Forest, Krishna Das, Kumea Sound, El Buho, Nick Barbachano, Jaya Lakshmi, Carbon Based Life Forms, Jonathan Goldman, Paul Temple, Deva Premal, Donna De Lory, Mirabai Ceiba, Snatam Kaur, Ajeet Kaur, Bird Tribe, Ayla Nereo, Ali Maya, Danit. Be sure to explore playlists on Spotify using keywords Tantra, Sensual, Romantic, Ceremony, Psychedelic and artist names. Also use keywords Prati music, RTT KAT, John Hopkins Psilocybin, MAPS music for more playlists in Spotify.

Sound Healing Education and tools

Serenity Tibet Healing bowls and tuning forks. Visit: https://www.serenityti-bet.com/

Jonathan Goldman Sound Healer Education and music: https://www.healing-sounds.com/

Kimba Arem Sound Healing: https://gaearth.com/

Paul Temple Sound Healing: https://www.radiancematrix.com/

Sacred Geometry Forms:

Greg Hoag's Sacred geometric forms and education: https://iconnect2all.com/

Buddha Maitreya Forms: https://www.buddhamaitreya.org/activities/monastic-meditation-tools/explore#!/~/search

www.ingramcontent.com/pod-product-compliance
Lightning Source LLC
Chambersburg PA
CBHW071713120626
46550CB00001B/220